Social Tourism

Social tourism refers to facilitating access to tourism for low income groups and/or the use of tourism as a regeneration and economic stimulation strategy. Although social tourism has its roots in the early 20th Century and is still a major component of the tourism sector in a range of countries, the concept has received relatively little research attention until recently. In this volume, international specialists on social tourism present perspectives on social tourism from different disciplines and geographical contexts. The book highlights the multitude of interpretations and implementations of social tourism that make the concept so multi-faceted: examples reviewed in this book include holiday vouchers in Hungary, charity initiatives in the UK, tourism schemes for senior citizens in Spain and state provision in Brazil.

Seven themed chapters and two case studies explore the potential of social tourism from a range of perspectives. Should tourism be a right that is available to all? Is social tourism indispensable in a sustainable tourism strategy? What are the different systems of social tourism supply and demand in Europe, and why do the implementations differ so much between countries? The book provides a critical reflection on these and other questions, and is therefore a key resource for social tourism researchers and practitioners.

This book was originally published as a special issue of *Current Issues in Tourism*.

Dr. Lynn Minnaert is a lecturer of Tourism and Events at the University of Surrey, UK.

Professor Robert Maitland is a Professor of City Tourism at the University of Westminster, UK.

Professor Graham Miller is the Head of the School of Hospitality and Tourism Management at the University of Surrey, UK.

Together they are the convenors of the seminar series NET-STaR (Network for Social Tourism and Regeneration), funded by the Economic and Social Research Council.

Social Tourism

Perspectives and Potential

Edited by
**Lynn Minnaert, Robert Maitland and
Graham Miller**

Routledge
Taylor & Francis Group

LONDON AND NEW YORK

First published 2013
by Routledge
2 Park Square, Milton Park, Abingdon, Oxon, OX14 4RN

Simultaneously published in the USA and Canada
by Routledge
711 Third Avenue, New York, NY 10017

Routledge is an imprint of the Taylor & Francis Group, an informa business

This book is a reproduction of *Current Issues in Tourism*, vol. 14, issue 5. The Publisher requests to those authors who may be citing this book to state, also, the bibliographical details of the special issue on which the book was based.

British Library Cataloguing in Publication Data
A catalogue record for this book is available from the British Library

ISBN13: 978-0-415-52378-3

Typeset in Times New Roman
by Saxon Graphics Ltd, Derby

Publisher's Note
The publisher would like to make readers aware that the chapters in this book may be referred to as articles as they are identical to the articles published in the special issue. The publisher accepts responsibility for any inconsistencies that may have arisen in the course of preparing this volume for print.

Contents

Citation Information   vii

1   Introduction
    Lynn Minnaert, Robert Maitland and Graham Miller   1

2   What is social tourism?
    Lynn Minnaert, Robert Maitland and Graham Miller   5

3   Systems of social tourism in the European Union: a critical review
    Anya Diekmann and Scott McCabe   19

4   Towards a 'tourism for all' policy for Ireland: achieving real sustainability
    in Irish tourism
    Kevin Griffin and Jane Stacey   33

5   The role of charities in social tourism
    Philippa Hunter-Jones   47

6   Social tourism in Hungary: from trade unions to cinema tickets
    László Puczkó and Tamara Rátz   61

7   Away from daily routines – holiday as a societal norm and a manifestation
    of an unequal society
    Minna Ylikännö   77

8   Accessible social tourism as a social policy strategy for healthy ageing: the
    relationship between tourism and functional health in older adults
    S. Carretero, M. Ferri, and J. Garcés   89

9   Case study: The International Organisation of Social Tourism (ISTO)
    working towards a right to holidays and tourism for all
    Charles Étienne Bélanger and Louis Jolin   103

CONTENTS

10 Case study: The development of social tourism in Brazil
      Marcelo Vilela de Almeida   111

      Index   119

Citation Information

The following chapters were originally published in *Current Issues in Tourism*, volume 14, issue 5 (July 2011). When citing this material, please use the original page numbering for each article, as follows:

Chapter 2
What is social tourism?
Lynn Minnaert, Robert Maitland and Graham Miller
Current Issues in Tourism, volume 14, issue 5 (July 2011) pp. 403–416

Chapter 3
Systems of social tourism in the European Union: a critical review
Anya Diekmann and Scott McCabe
Current Issues in Tourism, volume 14, issue 5 (July 2011) pp. 417–430

Chapter 4
Towards a 'tourism for all' policy for Ireland: achieving real sustainability in Irish tourism
Kevin Griffin and Jane Stacey
Current Issues in Tourism, volume 14, issue 5 (July 2011) pp. 431–444

Chapter 5
The role of charities in social tourism
Philippa Hunter-Jones
Current Issues in Tourism, volume 14, issue 5 (July 2011) pp. 445–458

Chapter 6
Social tourism in Hungary: from trade unions to cinema tickets
László Puczkó and Tamara Rátz
Current Issues in Tourism, volume 14, issue 5 (July 2011) pp. 459–473

Chapter 9
The International Organisation of Social Tourism (ISTO) working towards a right to holidays and tourism for all
Charles Étienne Bélanger and Louis Jolin
Current Issues in Tourism, volume 14, issue 5 (July 2011) pp. 475–482

Chapter 10
The development of social tourism in Brazil
Marcelo Vilela de Almeida
Current Issues in Tourism, volume 14, issue 5 (July 2011) pp. 483–90

Introduction

Lynn Minnaert , Robert Maitland and Graham Miller

Social tourism research, at least in the academic literature in English, has gone through a period of rapid development in the past 5 to 10 years. From a subject that was addressed but sporadically, it has received increasing levels of attention from researchers, resulting in a growing number of publications and a higher profile in tourism studies. The fact that this collection of papers, drawing on a special issue of the journal *Current Issues in Tourism*, has been selected to be enhanced and published as a research volume, is a testament to the more prominent position social tourism now takes in academic tourism research.

The editors of this volume first published about social tourism in 2007, and have witnessed the changing position of the research area first-hand since then. At the start of their research into social tourism, the available research showed a focus on non-participation (for example Haukeland, 1990) and the meaning of tourism for disadvantaged groups (for example Smith & Hughes, 1999) – but it should be emphasised that even these themes were but scarcely researched. Sources specifically on social tourism were even rarer (for example Hazel, 2005). The editors' first article (Minnaert et al., 2007) aimed to address this gap by examining the ethical foundations of social tourism, and addressing the question of why social tourism was supported by public funding in some societies, whereas in others this was not the case. In countries like France, Belgium, Portugal and Spain for example, the public sector is a major stakeholder in social tourism provision, whereas in countries like the United Kingdom and Ireland public sector support for social tourism policies is all but non-existent. On the basis of this study, the editors subsequently investigated the value of social tourism in social policy, in terms of potential increases to the social and family capital of low-income groups (Minnaert et al., 2009). This study examined the impacts of social tourism on low-income families in the short and medium term, and drew initial conclusions about the costs and benefits of social tourism compared to other forms of intervention. A study by McCabe (2009) also highlighted the potential outcomes of social tourism participation for socially excluded families. Their most recent article (Minnaert et al., 2011), included in this volume, builds on previous research and compares different implementations of social tourism – thus developing the first model of social tourism types. This article also addresses the question of the extent to which a 'right' to social tourism exists – 'right' is a term the European Union in particular is prone to use as a justification for encouragement of and investment into social tourism provision (for example in EESC, 2006). This discussion, together with a range of other research topics that are represented in this volume, illustrates the extent to which social tourism research has widened and deepened in recent years. Social tourism has developed into a research topic with a developing canon that is being investigated by authors from various countries and disciplines (also exemplified by McCabe et al., 2011).

Social tourism research has recently also been able to engage practitioners and policy makers – the potential of social tourism as a social and economic regeneration policy for the United Kingdom for example is currently being explored through two initiatives. The first is the All Party Parliamentary Group on Social Tourism, established in December 2010 under the chairmanship of Paul Maynard, Conservative MP for Blackpool North and Cleveleys. The purpose of this group is to investigate and promote the social and economic benefits of social tourism. Membership of APPGs has to be cross-party and the social tourism group includes MPs and Peers from the Conservative, Liberal Democrat and Labour parties. The APPG conducted the first Parliamentary enquiry into social tourism in the UK – evidence provided by the editors and several other authors in this volume was extensively used to shape the report resulting from this enquiry (APPG Social Tourism, 2011).

A second initiative that links social tourism to practitioners and policy makers is NET-STaR, the Network for Social Tourism and Regeneration. This network is run by the editors of this volume, and was funded by the Economic and Social Research Council – this can be seen as another indication of how social tourism has developed into a prominent and acknowledged research field. NET-STaR's objective is to create a network to explore the potential of social tourism as a regeneration strategy in the UK, drawing on scholarship from tourism, family and social policy, regeneration and spatial planning. The network brings together academics, policymakers and industry figures to examine existing academic work and to debate policy experiences. It was based on a series of six seminars, which aim to identify new research directions and point to innovative policy that is underpinned by theoretically informed research, collaborative in its approach, and cost-effective (www. westminster.ac.uk/net-star).

It is within this context of continued growth and development that the current volume has been created. It brings together perspectives and case studies of social tourism from different parts of the world, with examples of national initiatives, international comparisons and global organisations. It draws on the rich history of social tourism in Europe, and explores more recent manifestations and adaptations in non-European settings, such as Brazil. It consists of seven research papers and two case studies. Although much of the text is drawn from the special issue of *Current Issues in Tourism*, two new contributions have been added that highlight the continually expanding research activity around the subject.

The chapter by Minnaert, Maitland and Miller investigates different types of social tourism provision and sets out the connections and tensions between them in a social tourism model. The model compares the tourism product offered and the target groups that social initiatives are aimed at, creating a conceptual model that links social tourism types to the economic and social impacts they are likely to produce.

Diekmann and McCabe provide examples of different definitions and implementations of social tourism in the European context. Their chapter includes examples from Belgium, France, Germany, Poland, the UK, Romania and Spain. It considers the relationship of the social tourism sector and the commercial tourism sector in these different contexts and examines the impacts on employment. The authors argue that social tourism in Europe can represent an awkward mix of social liberalism on the one hand and concerns for propping up an important sector of the European economy (the mainstream tourism industry) on the other. They conclude however those social and economic developments do not necessarily need to be mutually exclusive.

Examples of other European countries are presented in the chapters of Griffin and Stacey, and Puzcó and Rátz. Griffin and Stacey's chapter examines the context for social tourism in Ireland, where, in contrast to many countries of mainland Europe, the concept of social tourism is still largely unfamiliar, and social tourism practices are mainly in the hands of voluntary and religious organisations. The authors analyse the policy aims of the Irish government with regards to sustainable tourism, and argue that environmental sustainability has hereby received a disproportionate emphasis, potentially at the expense of social sustainability. Social tourism is presented as a potential vehicle for economic and sustainable tourism development.

Puzcó and Rátz analyse the case of Hungary, where, in contrast with Ireland, social tourism has a long history starting in the communist era. The chapter discusses the developments in social tourism since the 1990s: much of the infrastructure that was originally owned by trade unions and companies was privatised or sold, and a holiday voucher scheme was introduced. The holiday vouchers provide access to tourism to a wide range of social groups, not simply those who could otherwise not afford to travel. The value of social tourism in terms of economic development and renewal is thus a key justification for provision.

Hunter-Jones's chapter focuses on the social tourism context in the UK, where provision is mainly in the hands of the charitable sector. The author discusses the fundamental role charities play in access to holidays for disadvantaged people, but shows that this function can at present be perceived as rather fragmented and uncoordinated. The chapter suggests closer cooperation between the voluntary and the private sectors, so that the needs of the target groups can be met more consistently. As state support for social tourism in the UK is currently argued to be unlikely, the trend towards a greater emphasis on Corporate Social Responsibility in the private sector may provide opportunities for more widespread provision.

The chapter by Ylikännö investigates the links between participation in tourism and perceived social status. It is a clear example of the cross-disciplinary nature of current social tourism research: it reviews holidays from a time-use perspective. The study analyses data from the International Social Survey Programme (ISSP) 2007 with a focus on leisure time and sports, and examines the extent to which holidays affect people's judgments about their position and status in society.

Carretero, Ferri and Garcés focus on the potential health benefits of tourism for older people, a growing group in contemporary society. This chapter reports the findings of a pilot study which compares the health and independence of travelling and non-travelling adults of 65 years old and over. The study highlights correlations between holiday taking and functional health and well-being in the sample group.

Two shorter case studies are presented in this volume: one considers the role of the International Social Tourism Organisation, and one discusses social tourism provision in Brazil. The first case study, by Bélanger and Jolin, explores the historical development of social tourism from the point of view of its main membership organisation, ISTO (International Social Tourism Organisation). Established in Brussels in 1963 as BITS (Bureau International du Tourisme Social, or International Bureau of Social Tourism), this organisation aimed to provide an international platform for the discussion of social tourism issues, and still plays this role today. The evolution of social tourism has meant that the organisation has gone through profound changes since its early beginnings: as social tourism moved away from its socio-educational, even socio-political origins and started to incorporate new target groups, BITS has kept abreast of these developments by introducing new objectives and directions. Bélanger and Jolin's case study explores the history of ISTO and the current and future challenges for the organisation.

The second case study, by Almeida, situates social tourism in the socio-economic and political context of Brazil, where the public sector can indeed be seen as the main stakeholder, even though the activities of voluntary organisations also play an important role. It discusses the challenges in implanting social tourism initiatives in a recently developed country, where a much bigger proportion of the population is excluded from tourism for economic reasons.

This book, the first in English to bring together social tourism research papers from a range of geographical and disciplinary perspectives, represents a succinct introduction to this vibrant and constantly developing field of enquiry.

References

All Party Parliamentary Group on Social Tourism (2011). *Giving Britain a break: Enquiry into the social and economic benefits of social tourism*. London: APPG Social Tourism.

Haukeland, J. (1990). Non-travellers. The flip side of motivation. *Annals of Tourism Research, 17*, 172–184.

Hazel, N. (2005). Holidays for families in need: A review of the research and policy context. *Children and Society, 19*(3), 225–236.

European Economic and Social Committee. (2006). *Opinion of the Economic and Social Committee on social tourism in Europe*. Brussels: EESC.

McCabe, S. (2009). Who needs a holiday? Evaluating social tourism. *Annals of Tourism Research, 36*(4), 667–688.

McCabe S., Minnaert, L., & Diekmann, A. (Eds) (2011). *Social tourism in Europe*. Bristol: Channel View Publications.

Minnaert, L., Maitland, R., & Miller, G. (2007). Social tourism and its ethical foundations. *Tourism Culture & Communication, 7*, 7–17.

Minnaert, L., Maitland, R., & Miller, G. (2009). Tourism and social policy. *Annals of Tourism Research, 36*(2), 316–334.

Minnaert, L., Maitland, R., & Miller, G. (2011). What is social tourism? *Current Issues in Tourism, 5*, 403–415.

Smith, V., & Hughes, H. (1999) Disadvantaged families and the meaning of the holiday. *International Journal of Tourism Research, 1,* 123–133.

www.westminster.ac.uk/net-star

What is social tourism?

Lynn Minnaert[a], Robert Maitland[b] and Graham Miller[a]

[a]School of Hospitality and Tourism Management, University of Surrey, Guildford GU2 7XH, UK;
[b]Centre for Tourism Research, University of Westminster, 35 Marylebone Road, London NW1 5LS, UK

This article examines the definitions and implementations of the concept of 'social tourism' that are in use in Europe today. Examples show that the concept has been implemented in many different ways to suit national contexts and that the justifications and goals of social tourism can differ greatly. The question arises how one can define the boundaries of this versatile and complex concept. This article proposes a model to clarify the interrelationships between the different interpretations: it highlights where common ground exists, but also where contradictions are apparent. The model consists of four main categories: the participation model, the inclusion model, the adaptation model and the stimulation model. The model draws on the historical development of social tourism and the ethical foundations for provision, and it is supported by a range of examples of European practice. Through this sub-categorisation of the concept, it is argued that a 'scientification' of the concept of social tourism can take place, so that the term does not lose its academic and political value. This article concludes by proposing a definition for social tourism that can effectively set the concept apart from other forms of tourism with attached social benefits.

Introduction

The current economic climate has raised questions in many parts of the world about the role of the state in providing social security and public welfare. UK Prime Minister David Cameron's ideas about a 'Big Society' are just one example of how governments may look for alternative ways to provide these services, by engaging local communities, charities and volunteering organisations. The purpose of the 'Big Society' is to find solutions to social problems 'from the bottom up', borne from the views and actions of the community itself rather than from the local or central government – and to reduce the welfare budget in the process. In the 'Big Society', the state moves from the position of a protectionist welfare state (pejoratively referred to as 'nanny state') to an enabling and accountable state, defined by transparency, payment by results and support for social enterprise and coopera-tives. In his speech in November 2009, David Cameron discussed how he proposed to decentralise power from the government to local communities and social entrepreneurs. He stated that 'this decentralisation of power from the central to the local will not just increase responsibility, it will lead to innovation, as people have the freedom to try new approaches to solving social problems, and the freedom to copy what works elsewhere' (Conservatives, 2011). In keeping with this flexible approach, governments are increasingly looking for alternative ways to deliver welfare results and to reduce the cost of providing benefits.

One potential measure to achieve social benefits in this way is social tourism. In several countries of the European Union, social tourism is provided at either very limited cost to the state or in ways which simultaneously stimulate the local economy and increase the income of the state via taxation and a reduction of unemployment benefits. This issue of *Current Issues in Tourism* reviews examples from a range of different countries and shows how the concept has been implemented in different ways to suit national contexts. Not only the implementations, but also the justifications and goals of social tourism can differ greatly. The development of the working classes, better health for inner city children, wider access to the benefits of tourism, loyalty to unions or companies and economic development of regions have all been, and in some cases are still, seen as valid reasons for provision.

If the examples presented here are so diverse, the question arises how one can define the boundaries of this versatile and complex concept. This special issue brings together perspectives and case studies of social tourism from different parts of the world, with examples of national initiatives, international comparisons and global organisations. It draws on the rich history of social tourism in Europe and explores more recent manifestations and adaptations in non-European settings, such as Brazil. The multi-faceted aspect of social tourism makes the phenomenon a difficult concept to define: with initiatives ranging from voucher schemes and government intervention to charitable holiday provision and social enterprise, what exactly is social tourism?

This article will explore different ways in which social tourism has come to be seen. It will highlight where common ground exists and where contradictions are apparent. It will propose a model that represents the different facets of social tourism as it exists today and provide a rationale for how these interpretations have been developed and justified. It will argue that as the conceptualisations of social tourism have developed, the term has become ever more elastic to incorporate all the different manifestations, so that it risks losing its clarity and credibility at a political and policy level and in academic discussion. Finally, suggestions will be offered for further research and a more nuanced understanding of the phenomenon of social tourism in the future.

Definitions and interpretations

The earliest definition of social tourism by Hunzicker (1951) describes social tourism as 'the relationships and phenomena in the field of tourism resulting from participation in travel by economically weak or otherwise disadvantaged elements in society' (p. 1). In 1957, Hunzicker added a comment regarding the nature of social tourism provision, defining the concept as 'a particular type of tourism characterised by the participation of people with a low income, providing them with special services, recognised as such' (Hunzicker, 1957, p. 12). These two early definitions highlight the complexity of the concept of social tourism, as they allow for four different interpretations. Each of these four interpretations is apparent in social tourism schemes in Europe today:

- *Social tourism is tourism that specifically encourages the participation in tourism activities of persons who are economically weak or otherwise disadvantaged.* Social tourism initiatives in this category aim to offer tourism experiences that are already accessible to a majority of persons to groups who are excluded from them, usually for financial or health reasons. The product offered is thus a standard product, the same product as is available to non-social tourism users. The disadvantaged are especially and actively targeted to encourage participation: examples include children with disabilities or senior citizens with complex health needs. Eligible groups may vary over time and between societies. These types of initiatives will be referred to as the *participation model.*

- *Social tourism is tourism that encourages participation in tourism by all, including persons who are economically or otherwise disadvantaged.* In this category, social tourism initiatives aim to encourage tourism participation for many or most members of the society – for example, through subsidised schemes such as holiday vouchers. Such initiatives see assistance to participate in tourism as a universal benefit, but with particular benefit to the economically least well off. The tourism product offered is again standard, the same for disadvantaged and non-disadvantaged groups. These types of initiatives will be referred to as the *inclusion model.*

- *Social tourism is tourism that is specifically designed for persons who are economically or otherwise disadvantaged.* These social tourism initiatives offer a product that is specifically adapted for social tourism users, for example, through the selection of specialist accommodation or the provision of support services. These could include facilities for persons with mobility problems or the organisation of specially designed activities to achieve particular social benefits. Participation in this type of social tourism is limited to the targeted users. These types of initiatives will be referred to as the *adaptation model.*

- *Social tourism is tourism that provides economic opportunities via travel and tourism for persons who are economically weak or otherwise disadvantaged.* In this interpretation, social tourism initiatives are mainly focused on providing economic benefits for the host community. The target users are seen as any potential client group that can be attracted during the shoulder season and increase sales and employment opportunities in the destinations. Certain social tourism users, such as senior citizens, can be an example of such a client group. A specific social tourism product (such as an all-inclusive group holiday) is proposed to attract participants in these initiatives, but selection criteria for participation are less rigid, as the schemes welcome both those who cannot participate in commercial tourism and those who can, but who opt for social tourism schemes instead. These types of initiatives will be referred to as the *stimulation model.*

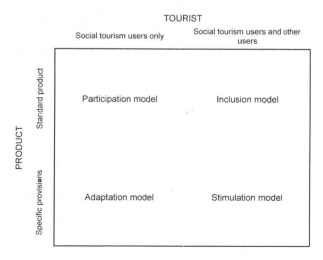

Each of the above interpretations finds an expression in social tourism practices today. In the *participation* model, social tourism is clearly targeted towards socially or otherwise disadvantaged persons in the society, but it is not necessarily characterised by specialised products or services. An example of this approach is the Centre for Holiday Participation in Flanders, Belgium. To increase the participation in tourism of low-income groups, the Centre negotiates reduced tariffs with accommodation providers and tourist attractions. These discounts are offered on a voluntary basis by the private sector in exchange for increased business, added publicity and in consideration of corporate social responsibility objectives. The discounted products are only available for persons on low incomes – their income status is either confirmed by a support worker in the social sector or beneficiaries provide a proof of their income themselves. The key characteristics of this approach to social tourism are that the product offered is *standard*, and no different from the experience offered outside of the scheme, and that participation in the programme is *limited to social tourism users*.

The *inclusion* model is also based on tourism products and services that are *standard* (the same for all participants, disadvantaged or not), but here the programme is *not limited to disadvantaged target groups*. An example of this interpretation of social tourism is the 'Chèques Vacances' (Holiday Voucher) scheme in France. Companies participating in this scheme give their employees the opportunity of making regular savings for their holiday, and these savings are supplemented by the employers and social organisations. The companies and social organisations benefit from reduced taxes and social contributions, which in effect constitute a state subsidy, funded by tax payers. (The 'Chèques Vacances' system however also creates an income stream for the public sector, as a commission is charged when the cheques are issued and banked.) The employee can redeem the total value of the savings and supplementary contributions in the form of holiday vouchers, which can be used on a wide variety of items including lodgings, dining, transport, leisure and culture. This system aims to enable access to holidays to the greatest number and is open to everyone irrespective of income. A motivation for making the system available to a wide range of employees is the economic impact of the holiday vouchers on the domestic tourism industry: it is estimated that total spending is four times more than the volume of vouchers issued (Minnaert, Quinn, Griffen, & Stacey, 2010). In this issue, Puszco and Ratz discuss a similar voucher scheme in Hungary.

The *adaptation* model applies to programmes that offer a product with *special provisions* for social tourism users, which is thus specifically adapted to the needs of disadvantaged target groups, and where participation is *limited to these disadvantaged target groups*. An example of this form of social tourism is Break, a charity in the UK providing short breaks and holidays for families with children with learning difficulties. The charity has four holiday centres where care staff are available to provide specialist care, and the centres have facilities for children with associated physical disabilities and high-level care needs (www.break-charity.org). The holidays are offered at reduced prices: the holiday makers pay around half of the cost, and the charity's fundraising activities cover the other half of the stay. Other programmes in the adaptation model may focus on different target groups, such as senior citizens (e.g. National Benevolent Fund for the Aged, UK), children with long-term illnesses (e.g. Fondation de France, France), single-parent families (e.g. One Parent Families, UK) or teenage parents (e.g. CRZ, Belgium).

The *stimulation model* differs significantly from the ones described above, as in this model the social benefits created for the destination are a key motivation for provision. Destinations or providers in this category are often affected by a decline in popularity and faced with spare capacity, particularly during the shoulder season, resulting in a lack of revenue and the need to terminate employment contracts. By attracting social tourism customers with specialised products during the shoulder season, a new market is created – initiatives of this type thus have economic as well as social benefits. An example of such a scheme is the IMSERSO programme in Spain. This programme offers dedicated holidays for senior citizens in coastal areas of Spain during the shoulder season. The holidays are financed through contributions by beneficiaries (70% in a single payment) and the public sector (30% of cost). The holiday offer is only available to senior citizens and includes transport, meals and activities. The state aims to recover its contribution through cost savings and earnings: the scheme allows for longer seasons and increased employment in the coastal regions, and the tourist expenditure may lead to higher tax income. Because of these factors, in addition to the potential social benefits for the participants, the contribution of the state is argued to be far outweighed by the financial benefit of the scheme (Minnaert et al., 2010). Around 300 hotels participate in the scheme, which has benefited around 1 million participants in the 2008–2009 season and has been estimated to generate or maintain 79,300 jobs. The Spanish government has allocated 105 million Euros for the 2009–2010 season, and it claims that every Euro invested yields 4 Euros in tax, spending and reduction in benefit payments (Imserso, 2011).

The stimulation model described above refers to schemes where the product offered is characterised by specialised services aimed at social tourism users, who cannot travel in the commercial circuit, and other users. There are also initiatives that aim to benefit the host region and thus show similarities to the stimulation model, though without focusing specifically on tourists with these characteristics. Examples are pro-poor tourism initiatives that aim to reduce poverty at the destination level by offering employment through tourism initiatives – the tourists visiting these initiatives are usually not poor or otherwise disadvantaged. Pro-poor tourism and community-based tourism could thus be seen as sub-categories of social tourism: this view is supported by ISTO, the International Social Tourism Organisation. ISTO defines social tourism as 'the effects and phenomena resulting from the participation in tourism, more specifically the participation of low-income groups. This participation is made possible or is facilitated by initiatives of a well-defined social nature' (ISTO, 2003). Even though the wording of the definition may be similar to those of Hunzicker, ISTO's interpretation of the low-income groups that participate in social tourism is broader: ISTO proposes that social tourism should benefit low-income persons not only by facilitating travel opportunities, but also by extending the benefits of tourism development to low-income persons at the destination level. In this issue, Bélanger and Jolin discuss how ISTO has adopted different terms for the two interpretations: the former interpretation of social tourism is referred as 'Tourism for All' and the latter as 'Solidarity Tourism'.

In an attempt to cover the different types of social tourism, each with its own target audience, product type, projected outcomes and motivations, Minnaert, Maitland and Miller (2007, 2009) defined social tourism as 'tourism with an added moral value, of which the primary aim is to benefit either the host or the visitor in the tourism exchange'. This definition makes a similar distinction as ISTO between initiatives that mainly aim to increase participation in tourism for disadvantaged groups and those that mainly aim to increase the economic benefits of tourism for disadvantaged groups. These two forms are defined as visitor-related and host-related social tourism. This definition acknowledges how the aims of social tourism can be applied to both visitors and hosts, but it still emphasises the foundation of social tourism to be social development – the social benefits of social tourism are described as their 'primary aim'. In this way, social tourism is distinguished from other forms of tourism that aim to stimulate regions economically. Although all economic regeneration initiatives can be seen to have social impacts, not all of these can be referred to as social tourism, and the above definition emphasises this. In the case of social tourism, the social impacts should be the primary intention of the scheme, rather than just one of the outcomes.

The model proposed in this article offers a visual representation of the different types of social tourism models in operation in Europe today, but, of course, the boundaries between different categories can be blurred. Clearly, many social tourism initiatives have economic as well as social aims, such as the French and Flemish examples as mentioned above which illustrate how the participation and inclusion models are focused on the increased participation in tourism, but simultaneously stimulate the local tourism sector as the initiatives only offer tourism products in their own country/own region. The model thus emphasises the primary motivations of initiatives, but secondary motivations may also be at play. An illustration of this is the IMSERSO example discussed as part of the stimulation model: even though economic aims are key motivations for the existence of the programme, part of its justification is that it provides a specialised holiday product for a potentially socially excluded group: senior citizens. From this point of view, the programme could be perceived as sharing characteristics with the adaptation model. The fact that the programme provides opportunities for social integration via travel and tourism makes public subsidy to a particular part of a particular industry (mainly hotels in coastal resorts) more acceptable – without this element, the initiative could be seen as unfair boosterism. The social aims of the IMSERSO programme though can be seen as secondary to the economic aims: this is illustrated by the fact that the selection criteria for the target users for this scheme are rather broadly defined. Every person over the age of 65 is eligible for state support, whereas not everyone in this group can be classified as economically disadvantaged or socially excluded. Although the scheme thus by nature follows a stimulation model, it is often presented as an adaptation programme, even if it has very little in common with other initiatives in this category. This illustrates how conflicting interpretations of social tourism can lead to tensions and unclear boundaries within the concept: as the term can be understood in many different ways, and each form has its own impacts and characteristics, two persons discussing 'social tourism' may be talking about entirely different schemes, making it hard to find common ground. The ethical justifications for running the schemes, and the social and economic impacts they generate, can differ greatly between the different examples. The following sections will examine these ethical justifications and impacts in more detail.

Ethical justifications: is tourism a right or a luxury?

Haulot (1982, p. 208), like Minnaert et al. (2007, 2009), includes a moral aspect in the definition of social tourism: 'Social tourism … finds justification in that its individual and collective objectives are consistent with the view that all measures taken by modern society should ensure more justice, more dignity and improved enjoyment of life for all citizens'. The view that social tourism is something modern societies 'should ensure' can be linked to the interpretation of social tourism as an expression of a 'right' to tourism – a principle that is advocated in a number of countries in Europe. The European Economic and Social Committee (EESC, 2006) in its 'Opinion of Social Tourism' defines social tourism explicitly as a right:

> Everyone has the right to rest on a daily, weekly and yearly basis, and the right to the leisure time that enables them to develop every aspect of their personality and their social integration. Clearly, everyone is entitled to exercise this right to personal development. The right to tourism is a concrete expression of this general right, and social tourism is underpinned by the desire to ensure that it is universally accessible in practice. (p. 68)

Although the EESC may propose tourism as a right, the organisation does not have the legitimacy to accord this right on a European level. Indeed, access to tourism is by no means universally seen as a right: for many, it will rather be a luxury, a discretionary activity to which no right exists. If social tourism exists, should there also be social cars or social game consoles? Both examples can be argued to support social integration: the car can increase mobility, maybe increase employment opportunities and reinforce social networks. The game console can be seen as a valuable status symbol, and when asked, children may prefer it to a family holiday. So what sets a holiday apart from these other examples?

The ethical principles that are predominant in different societies may help to shed light on these questions. Almost all ethical theories agree that every citizen should have the same rights in the society and should be equal before the law. Nevertheless, they may differ on the issue of the duties that stronger strata in the society have towards the weaker. On the one hand, society can be seen as a combination of actors, whereby each actor is shaped by their environment – the performance of one member is intrinsically linked to that of the other members. From this perspective, societies where the stronger strata support the weaker will reduce the inequality between their members and thus become stronger overall. This view is predominant in what may be termed 'socialised' societies, often influenced by Christian or Marxist ethics (Minnaert et al., 2007). On the other hand, 'individualised' societies do not support the *a priori* duty of the stronger strata towards the weaker, but instead emphasise that the opportunities offered to one person should not limit the opportunities of another. Every member in the society should receive equal opportunities, but this does not mean that the inequality between members should be reduced *per se*. The morality of an action is determined by whether an individual can promote his or her own welfare, without hindering the opportunities of others (Minnaert et al., 2007).

These two views on the duties of the stronger strata towards the weaker may have implications for the subsequent views on social tourism: this can be seen as an *entitlement* (right) or a *desert*. George (1999, p. 35) defines entitlement as that 'based on the application of a rule according to its terms, without regard to individual qualities that the rule ignores'. In socialised societies where the reduction of inequality and the support of the weaker strata are seen as an *a priori* moral duty, social tourism could be more easily argued to be an entitlement. The entitlement exists without restrictions on those who qualify for it, the rule is universal: purely by being part of the disadvantaged, a person can be entitled to public support. This view can be linked to the classic European social model.

In individualised societies, where this *a priori* duty is weaker, social tourism could at best be argued to be a desert: George (1999, p. 34) defines this as an implication of moral responsibility, which presupposes freedom. Being part of a society comes with a number of moral responsibilities – only those who fulfil these responsibilities 'deserve' support. Whereas entitlement is universal, desert is not: it depends on the characteristics and behaviour of the person in question. A person who has been made redundant when a company closes down may be seen to 'deserve' benefits from the government for a limited period while looking for other employment: this is because the person has fulfilled his or her responsibility to the society by showing willingness and ability to work and by paying taxes while in employment. This does not mean that every person who is out of work is necessarily seen as equally 'deserving' of these benefits: the long-term unemployed, for example, may be seen by some as having lost their right to full benefits, by not fulfilling their duty to the society while unemployed. Desert is thus linked to individual qualities, which may mean that someone has 'deserved' a certain reward, whereas another person has not. This is more in line with the neo-liberal social model. In terms of social tourism, this means that whereas some individual cases may be deemed 'deserving' of social tourism, this cannot be seen as an entitlement based on a general rule.

Individualised societies are generally more resistant to the concept of entitlement than socialised societies, as the entitlement of one person can be argued to be a reduction of 'personal liberty' of the other. The concept of personal liberty though can be said to play an important role in both the individualised and the socialised perspective on society. Berlin (1958) discussed two concepts of liberty, positive and negative liberty. Negative liberty is referred to as the 'freedom from': persons are free if they can act and be as they choose without the interference of others. In individualised societies, this has resulted in the view that state intervention should be kept as minimal as possible so that every member of the society is free to develop as he or she chooses. Positive liberty though is referred to as 'freedom to': in this case, a just and fair society is one where its citizens are not prevented from developing into their 'ideal selves'. To achieve this society, persons with more opportunities to do this may need to make sacrifices to those with fewer opportunities to do so – this is a view pursued by more socialised societies.

Although the European social model is generally seen as an example of a socialised societal model, whereas the Anglo-Saxon social model can be seen as an example of the individualised societal model, the concept of 'desert' can be seen to be under closer scrutiny in both. Due to the deteriorated economic climate and the increased pressure on welfare budgets, the question of who deserves state help and who does not is becoming more prominent. This adds to a much older discussion about who are the 'deserving' and who are the 'undeserving' poor. Chunn and Gavigan (2004, p. 231) argue that a shift towards more neo-liberal policies has resulted in a 'huge expansion in the category of undeserving poor. Indeed, virtually no one is considered "deserving"; even those who do receive social assistance are viewed as temporary recipients who must demonstrate their willingness to work for welfare and who ultimately will be employed as a result of skills and experience gained through workfare and other government-subsidised programmes. Thus, sole-parent mothers who historically were more likely to be deemed "deserving" than were childless men and women are no longer so privileged'. Because fewer persons are seen as 'deserving', programmes to redistribute wealth can be reduced. The unpopularity of redistribution policies in individualised societies is by no means new: Will (1993, p. 313) highlight the 'strong public distaste' for welfare programmes in the USA 15 years ago. Recently though, socialised societies (e.g. Sweden) have moved towards more individualised attitudes towards the role of the government in social welfare and which elements of the welfare system can be seen as entitlements. In an economic climate where public spending is widely reduced, the criteria for what constitutes an entitlement become ever stricter. In this context, it is thus unlikely that the right to tourism will be easily accepted as an entitlement, although on the basis of utilitarian principles, it may be considered as a desert if the economic and social impacts of the intervention can be shown to outweigh the costs. In several countries of Europe, social tourism programmes have already been adapted in this direction, as is illustrated by Diekmann and McCabe in this issue.

The previous paragraph may go some way in explaining why tourism may be seen as a right more easily in certain societies than in others. Nevertheless, it does not answer the more fundamental question why there should exist a right to a holiday and tourism, rather than a right to a car or a game console. The European Economic and Social Committee (2006) sees tourism as a right on the basis of the benefits it can bring to both the participants and society in the wider sense: social tourism in its view contributes to social integration, to the creation of sustainable tourism structures, to employment and economic development at the destination level and to the so-called global development by offering an alternative to declining agriculture and manufacturing industries. Although there is a growing body of evidence that supports the existence of these benefits, one could argue that these benefits do not in themselves justify the denomination of tourism as an entitlement or a right, on the same level as healthcare and education – and even these two are contested in some societies. Entitlement is not dependent on the outcomes of the intervention, as it is 'based on the application of a rule according to its terms, without regard to individual qualities that the rule ignores' (George, 1999, p. 34). The social and economic benefits highlighted by the EESC underpin the provision of social tourism from a more utilitarian perspective: this perspective assesses policies on the basis of a cost–benefit analysis for the society as a whole. As utilitarian ethics are more common in individualised societies, it could be argued that they support the case for social tourism as a desert, as something that is 'good to have' for the society as a whole, but by themselves these benefits can be said not to justify social tourism as an entitlement or right.

Several articles in this issue argue that public sector bodies should increase their support of social tourism based on the benefits it can bring and its status as a potential 'desert' for certain groups in the society. Almeida discusses this in the context of Brazil, where social tourism is a more recent phenomenon than in Europe and where the public sector can indeed be seen as the main stakeholder, even though the activities of voluntary organisations also play an important role. Stacey and Griffen's article examines the context for social tourism in Ireland, where, in contrast to many countries of mainland Europe, the concept of social tourism is still largely unfamiliar, and social tourism practices are mainly in the hands of voluntary and religious organisations. The authors present social tourism as a potential vehicle for economic and social tourism development. Similar to Ireland, there is very little state involvement in social tourism in the UK. Hunter-Jones discusses the role that charities play in the access to holidays for disadvantaged persons. Charitable provision increases the welfare of the disadvantaged groups without hindering the opportunities of others and does not create entitlement: from this perspective, this is a typical example of social tourism provision in an individualised society.

Socio-economic justifications: potential impacts of social tourism

The provision of social tourism has been linked to and justified by both social and economic benefits. A growing body of research evidence indicates that social tourism can generate both types of benefits. Minnaert et al. (2009), Minnaert (2008) and McCabe (2009) have conducted research on the social impacts of participation in social tourism by low-income beneficiaries and have found evidence of benefits ranging from increases in self-esteem, improvement in family relations and widening of travel horizons to more pro-active attitudes to life and participation in education and employment. On an economic level, there is evidence that the development of social tourism can help to sustain jobs in the low season and generate income for host communities.

In recent interpretations of social tourism, the economic benefits of the phenomenon have started to play an ever more central role: they offer a financial, rather than purely moral, argument for social tourism development. This has resulted in a markedly increased interest in social tourism projects in the stimulation model. An example of this increased emphasis on the stimulation model is the Calypso programme of the European Commission for Enterprise and Industry. This programme aims to develop social tourism programmes and exchanges between different European countries. Four key target groups have been identified: senior citizens, families in difficult personal or financial circumstances, persons with disabilities and young people. The social aims of personal development, well-being, European citizenship and learning are highlighted, but the economic aims of the programme are more specifically defined. The programme aims to generate economic activity and growth across Europe, reduce seasonality, create and sustain more and better jobs in the tourism sector and assist in the development of small emerging destinations at a regional level (European Commission, 2011). In this programme, the emphasis on helping people with low incomes has almost entirely disappeared: even though it is still a criterion for the target group of 'families in difficult personal and financial circumstances', it is not explicitly mentioned for the other three categories. Not all senior citizens, young people and persons with disabilities are excluded from the tourism industry and the benefits of holidays without social tourism provision – the benefit of economic stimulation for the host community and the positive social impacts on the participants are seen as a justification to widen the target audience for social tourism initiatives.

The current economic climate, which has led to a number of governments reassessing their welfare programmes, may play a role in the increasing emphasis on the economic benefits of social tourism. Even in the current climate, social tourism schemes have not been abolished, on the contrary: the Calypso programme aims to develop social tourism – albeit mainly of one particular type – at a time when welfare spending is often under heightened scrutiny. The target groups for social tourism are not limited or reduced, they are extended: the Calypso programme has the objective to increase the uptake of social tourism initiatives by making them more widely known and available. The potential economic benefits of social tourism are highlighted as a key motivation for this development, but another factor also plays a role: the existing social tourism infrastructure in many European countries.

Traditional social tourism infrastructure in many countries of mainland Europe was based around the 'holiday centres'. These holiday centres were particularly popular between 1950 and 1980, because they represented a product that was new, desirable and affordable and helped towards democratisation of holiday making. Traditionally, they offered a stay in full board with all entertainment and activities included. In many cases, the sector had a socio-educational or even socio-political aspect. The organised activities on holiday were often inspired by the ideals of the popular educational movements and sometimes had a strong ideological character (Jolin, 2003). The holiday makers stayed in rather basic accommodation at low rates and often helped with the daily chores. Most holiday centres were run by charities, unions or companies. This might have been one of the reasons for their management becoming very bureaucratic over the years. Still, they developed according to the needs of their public: many switched from full board to half board, the visitors had more freedom when choosing their activities and help with the chores was no longer required (Chauvin, 2002, p. 67). It is certainly no coincidence that these changes occurred when commercial tourism became more accessible to people from weaker economic backgrounds. After 1980, social tourism faced a number of important challenges. This was mainly due to the changes affecting the traditional target group for social tourism, the manual workers: they were increasingly able to take holidays in the commercial circuit, because of the low prices that mass tourism could offer. Social tourism organisations, such as ISTO, have adapted to the changes in the market environment and have expanded their focus by adding Solidarity Tourism (see Belanger & Jolin, 2011) – as the demand for traditional social tourism product diminished, they extended their scope to demonstrate their continuing relevance.

Faced with the competition of mass tourism and the low prices offered, traditional social tourism establishments found it hard to match the prices of holidays abroad. As a result of this development, much of the social tourism infrastructure was privatised and sold (Puszco and Ratz discuss this development in Hungary in this issue). The infrastructure that remained has often had to adapt to self-sustain and remain relevant. Some countries, such as France and Belgium, provide limited state subsidies for these establishments: these are referred to as 'aide à la pierre' ('support for infrastructure', as opposed to 'aide à la personne', 'support for the holiday maker'). In recent years, there has been increased pressure on these traditional social tourism businesses to become less reliant on state support and diversify towards new products and new markets – and these pressures are increasing further now. In France, for example, it can be seen that many accommodation providers that originally catered for social tourism now mainly attract middle-class, older visitors (Caire, 2011). This means that the boundaries between social and commercial tourism have become increasingly blurred: in some countries, traditional social tourism providers have had to adapt to commercial demand and attract new customers, whereas in other countries, commercial businesses turn to social tourism to attract business in the low season (e.g. the IMSERSO programme in Spain).

It is important to highlight here that even though initiatives following the stimulation model may have a range of positive economic outcomes, they may perform less well in terms of social outcomes. Studies highlighting the positive social impacts of social tourism have not been carried out with stimulation schemes, but with initiatives in the adaptation and participation models – models that are focused exclusively on the needs of disadvantaged and socially excluded users. Minnaert et al. (2009) emphasised in their study of the outcomes of social tourism that positive outcomes were only reached if an adequate level of support could be provided to holiday makers: some holiday makers hardly need any support at all, but others may need help planning the transport, packing their luggage or finding things to do during their time away. The study also showed that support after the holiday may be equally important to harness the positive attitudes and motivation the holiday may have encouraged into the participation in courses, the search for specialised support or the search for employment. As initiatives in the stimulation category currently do not include any of these support initiatives, the social outcomes may be less significant than those of more tailored and specialised programmes. Justifying social tourism initiatives in the 'stimulation' category on the basis of the positive social outcomes of other types of programmes is thus only partially accurate: every programme should be evaluated individually, in terms of both economic and social outcomes.

Conclusions

This article has explored some of the definitions and interpretations of social tourism that are in use today. It has highlighted that there are tensions, and in some cases contradictions, between different interpretations of and motivations for social tourism. The beneficiaries of social tourism can differ greatly depending on the individual programmes considered: in some cases, they are confined to members of economically or otherwise disadvantaged groups; in other cases, the beneficiaries include, but are not restricted to, disadvantaged persons. In other cases still, the beneficiaries are not those who travel, but members of the host community. The motivations for provision are equally diverse: social tourism can be seen as the expression of a fundamental right to travel, as a vehicle for the economic development of regions, as a measure to increase social inclusion or as a route to greater European citizenship. It can be said that 'social tourism' has become an umbrella term for all these different expressions, and this article has proposed that the concept needs to be defined and nuanced more precisely through sub-categorisation. By examining the target users and the product offered in social tourism initiatives in Europe, the model proposes four main categories: the participation model, the inclusion model, the adaptation model and the stimulation model. Solidarity tourism, with its links to pro-poor tourism and community-based tourism, can be seen as a bridging model between social tourism and commercial tourism. On the basis of this model, the justifications and impacts of different types of social tourism can be compared, contrasted and evaluated for effectiveness.

Social tourism research is still in a relatively early stage, and further research is needed before a 'scientification' of the concept can take place. Jafari (2001) has explored how this 'scientification' developed for tourism studies, in itself a recent area of study. He discussed how knowledge and theory in the field of tourism, in general, have developed around four platforms: the advocacy, cautionary, adaptancy and knowledge-based platforms. A similar 'scientification' is noted by Hardy, Beeton and Pearson (2002), who have applied the idea to sustainable tourism. They challenge the vagueness of the concept by arguing that 'given the reactionary nature of sustainable tourism to current paradigmatic approaches and the difficulties associated with defining it, this leads to the question of whether sustainable tourism will be able to be developed theoretically and practically or is it simply reactionary rhetoric?' (Hardy et al., 2002, p. 490). In reaction to this conceptual challenge, it can be seen that 'sustainable tourism' is increasingly sub-categorised, critiqued and nuanced. Links have been built between sustainable tourism and eco-tourism, community-based tourism, responsible tourism and alternative tourism, to name but a few; yet each of these concepts commands a specific definition and is developing its own strand in the tourism literature. A similar development can be seen to have started in the case of social tourism, with concepts such as the four categories proposed in this article, host- and visitor-related social tourism, solidarity tourism and tourism for all as potential nuances.

If all the different forms of social tourism presented in this special issue are indeed expressions of the same concept, the concept perhaps needs to be more clearly defined and sub-categorised, so that it does not become a meaningless label. The question can be asked if a common definition of social tourism is at all possible, considering the different forms the concept can take, and if having this definition is desirable or unnecessarily limiting. The authors propose to define social tourism as 'tourism with an added moral value, of which the primary aim is to benefit either the host or the visitor in the tourism exchange'. Although a definition such as this one does not, in itself, do justice to the different manifestations of social tourism and their individual characteristics, it has the benefit of positioning social tourism against regeneration projects that can be seen as mainly economic. The range of interpretations of the concept underlies the wealth of examples described in this issue, and the proposed definition highlights the common ground between them.

References

Belanger, C.E., & Jolin, L. (2011). Case study: The International Organisation of Social Tourism (ISTO) working towards a right to holidays and tourism for all. *Current Issues in Tourism, 14*(5), 475–482.

Berlin, I. (1958). *Two concepts of liberty.* Oxford: Clarendon Press.

Caire, J. (2011). Social tourism and the social economy. In A. Diekmann, S. McCabe, & L. Minnaert (Eds.), *Social tourism in Europe.* Bristol: Channel View Publications, in press.

Chauvin, J. (2002). *Le tourisme social et associatif en France.* Paris: l'Harmattan.

Chunn, D., & Gavigan, S. (2004). Welfare law, welfare fraud and the moral regulation of the 'never deserving' poor. *Social & Legal Studies, 13,* 219–243.

Conservatives. 2011. Retrieved from http://www.conservatives.com/News/News_stories/2010/07/Our_Big_Society_Agenda.aspx.

European Commission. 2011. Retrieved from http://ec.europa.eu/enterprise/sectors/tourism/calypso/index_en.htm.

European Economic and Social Committee. (2006). *Opinion of the Economic and Social Committee on Social Tourism in Europe.* Brussels: EESC.

George, R. (1999). *In defence of natural law.* Oxford: Clarendon Press.

Hardy, A., Beeton, R., & Pearson, L. (2002). Sustainable tourism: An overview of the concept and its position in relation to conceptualisations of tourism. *Journal of Sustainable Tourism, 10*(6), 475–496.

Haulot, A. (1982). Social tourism: Current dimensions of future developments. *Journal of Travel Research, 20*(3), 207–212.

Hunziker, W. (1951). *Social tourism: Its nature and problems.* International Tourists Alliance Scientific Commission.

Hunzicker, W. (1957). Cio che rimarrebe ancora da dire sul turismo sociale. *Revue de tourisme, 2,* 52–57.

Imserso. 2011. Retrieved from http://www.imserso.es/imserso_06/index.htm.

ISTO. (2003). *Statutes.* Brussels: Author.

Jafari, J. (2001). The scientification of tourism. In V. Smith & M. Brent (Eds.), *Hosts and guests revisited: Tourism issues of the 21st Century* (pp. 211–220). New York, NY: Cognizant.

Jolin, L. (2003). Le tourisme social, un concept riche de ses évolutions. *Le tourisme social dans le monde.* Teoros 141, Edition spéciale 40ème anniversaire, i–xxi.

McCabe, S. (2009). Who needs a holiday? Evaluating social tourism. *Annals of Tourism Research, 36*(4), 667–688.

Minnaert, L. (2008). *Holidays are for everyone. Research into the effects and the importance of holidays for people living in poverty.* Brussels: Tourism Flanders. Retrieved from Tourism Flanders website http://www.holidayparticipation.be/downloads/tourism_research_notebook.pdf.

Minnaert, L., Maitland, R., & Miller, G. (2007). Social tourism and its ethical foundations. *Tourism Culture & Communication, 7,* 7–17.

Minnaert, L., Maitland, R., & Miller, G. (2009). Tourism and social policy – the value of social tourism. *Annals of Tourism Research, 36*(2), 316–334.

Minnaert, L., Quinn, B., Griffen, K., & Stacey, J. (2010). Social tourism for low-income groups: Benefits in a UK and Irish context. In S. Cole & N. Morgan (Eds.), *Tourism and inequality* (pp. 126–143). Wallingford: CABI.

Will, J. (1993). The dimensions of poverty: Public perceptions of the deserving poor. *Social Science Research, 22,* 212–232.

Systems of social tourism in the European Union: a critical review

Anya Diekmann[a] and Scott McCabe[b]

[a]IGEAT-LIToTeS, Faculté des Sciences, Université Libre de Bruxelles, av. Franklin Roosevelt 50, CP 130/02, B-1050, Brussels, Belgium; [b]Nottingham University Business School, Jubilee Campus, Wollaton Road, Nottingham NG8 1BB, UK

Recently, the European Commission (EC) has placed a focus on social tourism issues within Europe. The underlying logic of this intervention is that social tourism aims for social equity, aiding access to tourism to provide fair tourism for all citizens and contributing towards sustainability of the European tourism industry. By linking social tourism to sustainable development, the EC sets priorities for future policies to foster mobility within the community. Yet, most European countries have different approaches, priorities and diverse ideological interpretations of the role of the state in tourism provision. Consequently, systems and practices vary strongly between nations and seem to put the ideal of a common approach a very distant prospect. This paper outlines the context of these approaches to social tourism to highlight these challenges and to propose initiatives for the future integration of the European social tourism sector. It presents a comparative analysis of social tourism systems in seven European countries with important social tourism structures. The paper assesses different interpretations of social tourism, examining development and employment issues. In addition, the paper assesses the links with the commercial tourism sector and provides recommendations for future development in the social tourism sector and consequences for European policy.

Introduction

Social tourism has recently become a flagship tourism policy in the European Union (EU hereafter). Combining aspects of social integration, sustainability and economic regeneration, social tourism at its best represents the ideals, aims and objectives of a truly social Europe. For that reason, the European Commission (EC) focuses on social tourism issues by organising conferences, highlighting examples of best practices and launching research projects, such as the recent Calypso project (2009). Together with the objective of reducing seasonality issues in the tourism sector within member states, the aims of this scheme are to propose a mechanism for targeting social tourism consumers and to develop an implementation scheme to foster cross-national exchange. A key challenge to these aims lies in the diversity of approaches (and systems) of social tourism throughout

Europe, which impedes the quality of evidence concerning the needs and benefits of such activity.

Accompanying this diversity of approaches to social tourism is a lack of attention within the academic community. Although social tourism can trace its roots to the beginnings of modern tourism, it has received little attention from the academic world. Recent research in France and the UK has rekindled interest however (Caire, 2005; Hall & Brown, 2006; McCabe, 2009; Minnaert, Maitland, & Miller, 2007). The field lacks a single definition, thus research is often presented as a form of welfare tourism rather than being overtly linked to the concept of 'social tourism' (Abdel-Ghaffar, Handy, Jafari, Kreul, & Stivala, 1992; Hall & Brown, 1996; Jefferson, 1991). This lack of clarity is exacerbated by the fact that the concept of social tourism encompasses a broad range of activity, ensuring that there is often a poor level of knowledge or understanding about what social tourism means, despite valuable theorising, which posits social tourism either as a social force or as a tool to reduce inequality (Graburn, 1983; Higgins-Desbiolles, 2006; Krippendorf, 1987). There are also different ways of approaching social tourism. While much research takes a sociological approach, in France, the literature provides a more socio-economical and organisational analysis (Caire, 2005, 2006; Chauvin, 2002; La Documentation Française, 1992).

There is little seminal research, and much of what is available in the social tourism literature tends to present evidence from a single country perspective at the expense of cross-border comparative analyses. Comparisons are further impeded by a paucity in conjoined studies, with much research focusing on a specific target group such as: senior/youth tourism; low-income families or the disabled. Alongside the academic literature are numerous annual reports, market analyses undertaken by international and national social tourism organisations (for instance ISTO[1], Flanders Region, Floréal, UNAT[2], FHA[3]). Often these literatures do not intersect due to language and translation barriers. This represents a real gap in the knowledge of tourism particularly since social tourism is well established and deeply embedded with the framework of social democratic movements. The lack of transfer of knowledge between countries and between organisations/academia has reduced the level of overall impact of social tourism research on policy.

Therefore, the aim of the present paper is to begin to address these issues through a comparative analysis of diverse social tourism systems and practices including supply and demand (target groups) in seven European countries with important social tourism structures: Belgium, France, Germany, Poland, UK, Romania and Spain. The purpose is to propose a framework that would enable the development of a common approach for social tourism to be developed. The paper outlines different definitions and interpretations of social tourism and examines the systems in different countries. This is achieved through a discussion of the range of funding mechanisms, target groups (beneficiaries of social tourism), an assessment of the structures of supply and facilities, and finally an evaluation of the links with the commercial tourism sector. The paper draws largely on results of the recent study 'Employment in the European social tourism sector' (Diekmann, Duquesne, Maulet, & De Nicolo, 2009). This project undertaken for the ISTO and EFFAT (European Federation for Food, Agriculture and Tourism) focused on employment issues within the European social tourism sector. While the current paper does not wish to repeat those findings, the purpose is to develop a discussion based on key issues that arose as a consequence of the research. Finally, the paper concludes with a consideration of perspectives for future development in the social tourism sector and a reflection on the consequences for future European policy in this area.

Defining social tourism – European perspectives

Although 'social tourism' has existed as a concept at least for the last 60 years, its definition is still fuzzy and is interpreted differently in many countries. In 1957, Hunziker defined social tourism as a 'particular type of tourism characterised by the participation of people with a low income, providing them with special services, recognised as such' (Hunziker, 1957, p. 52). For Arthur Haulot (1982), the term means 'the totality of relations and phenomena deriving from the participation of those social groups with modest incomes – participation which is made possible or facilitated by measures of a well-defined social character' (Haulot, 1982, p. 208). While for Minneart, Maitland and Miller (2007) social tourism relates 'to an added moral value, which aims to benefit either the host or the visitor in the tourism exchange' (Minnaert et al., 2007, p. 9) thus presenting social tourism within an ethical position.

As competition has increased and led to a fragmentation of markets within the commercial sector, alongside changes in public sector funding for social care, the essence of social tourism appears to have changed in recent years. In the UK and Ireland, social tourism most often refers to the provision of access to tourism for disabled or otherwise disadvantaged families who could not possibly take a holiday (see McCabe, 2009), whereas on continental Europe, social tourism appears to focus on social cohesion or integration (*mixité sociale*) issues and the 'tourism for all' (TFA) agenda. TFA is a concept related to social tourism. While in Belgium, the term is integrative in the sense of addressing all individuals of the society, in Germany and in the UK for example, the term is used largely in the context of the integration of access for disabled people. The organisation 'Tourismus für alle' (Germany) refers purely to disabled people, one segment of the wider social tourism market. Mundt defines German social tourism as the 'deployment and grants through travel offers for people for whom travelling for recreational purposes is for any reason whatsoever outside their possibilities' (Mundt, 2004, p. 166) thus creating a differentiation between social tourism and 'tourism for all' which is not consistent across all European countries.

Along with commercial tourism, social tourism developed in the 1950s particularly in countries with well-developed social systems such France, Belgium, Germany, Spain and the Eastern European countries. The main organisers behind the social tourism movement were trade unions and welfare and health organisations. At the same time, international organisations promoting social tourism were set up, such as the Federation of Popular Travel Organisations (IFPTO) and the Federation of International Youth Travel Organisations (FIYTO) in 1950. At the Brussels international congress of social tourism in 1963, social tourism organisations together with the representatives of public authorities decided to create the BITS (Bureau International du Tourisme Social, recently changed to ISTO), whose aims are for common reflection, coordination and action. Over the past 50 years, several governments have integrated 'social tourism' into their social welfare policies, resulting in state-backed schemes to provide and promote affordable holidays and recreation.

Social tourism is often defined in contrast to commercial tourism. Couveia (1995) suggests that social tourism should be understood as a type of tourism whose main or exclusive characteristic should be a non-commercial goal. In Eastern Europe, the former socialist countries deployed the term to designate the whole of tourism activities. In the Democratic Republic of Germany (GDR), for instance, collective social tourism was coterminous to severe limitations placed on general freedoms to travel (Mundt, 2004). It was only with the arrival of the free market economy at the beginning of the 1990s that the 'social tourism model' developed into a 'commercial tourism model' in the GDR. Declining demand for mass tourism facilities forced an adaptation to the new rules of the free market system of global capitalism. Along with decreasing public funding and harsh price competition from the commercial tourism market, social tourism stakeholders in some countries, such as Belgium and France focused on quality issues and access to a broader public (Diekmann et al., 2009, p. 27). The boundaries between commercial and social tourism then became blurred.

From an economic point of view, social tourism is estimated by social tourism organisations such as the ISTO to play an important role notably in tourism employment. Yet, it is apparent that few countries in Europe collect statistics in a way that allows the disaggregation of social tourism activity from mainstream tourism, resulting in an inability to collect reliable data on the economic impact of social tourism. Only a few countries actively collect statistics resulting in inadequate data for international comparison. However, where statistics are collected, there are some useful trends highlighted. In France for instance, in 2003, UNAT estimated that 12% of the 45.4 million people going on a holiday were social tourists using social tourism infrastructures (Caire, 2005) and that about 10% of the whole accommodation sector was made up of social tourism stock (Caire, 2006). Social tourism is an important sector of the overall tourism economy in France, yet this is a result of an embedded system of financial support for social tourism which is integrated well when compared with many other counties.

The most well-known definition of social tourism originated from the Montreal Declaration on Social Tourism (1996), which forms the basis for article three of the ISTO statute, social tourism is: 'all of the relationships and phenomena resulting from participation in tourism, and in particular from the participation of social strata with modest incomes. This participation is made possible, or facilitated, by measures of a well-defined social nature' (BITS, 1996). This definition infers social/state support for a wide range of groups and is thus inclusive of TFA and a wide range of potential users. Furthermore, since the Palma conference organised by the Committee of Regions on Social Tourism in November 2005, sustainability has become an intrinsic aspect of social tourism. An example is the integration of social tourism issues in the policy remit of the Tourism Sustainability Group (TSG). In some countries such as Belgium there is an ongoing debate on the definition and image of social tourism, and while the adoption of TFA concerns have been positively welcomed, there have been doubts about the integration of the term sustainability as relevant to social tourism since these concepts potentially further blur boundaries and understanding about social tourism. It seems apparent that the lack of clear understanding and definition for social tourism has provided a hindrance to the development of integrative policies within Europe.

One definitional aspect that has been largely overlooked is the degree of public funding given to social tourism. This is often linked with a political/ideological desire to provide people with the means to benefit from what is argued to be their constitutional right to go on a holiday. With the exception of the UK, all countries under scrutiny in this paper have a public funding policy, even though levels of subsidies vary a great deal. Aside from the EU report of 1994 (Commission des Communautés Européennes – D.G. XXIII – Unité Tourisme, 1994), these funding systems have hardly ever been researched or their effectiveness compared. However, as argued in this paper, these issues cannot be separated from two important elements for tackling and understanding social tourism systems in the different countries. These are: the lack of a unified definition adopted by all countries in the EU; and the variation of target groups from one country to another. Finally, the term can have secondary meanings in some countries. For example, in Germany, 'Sozialtourismus' also refers to the migration of populations from poorer countries, but has hardly any connotation with tourism practices. Social tourism is also understood as a social action with a close link with volunteer tourism.

This indeterminacy of definitions is exacerbated by only a partial analysis within the academic study of social tourism, which despite a current resurgence of interest remains incomplete. Early research included considerations of the structural inequalities of access to tourism and cultural differences in attitudes and behaviours as a determining factor affecting participation (Richards, 1998, 1999), while the major strands of research on social tourism in the English language has focused on the benefits of participation (Hazel, 2005; Hunter-Jones, 2004) or access barriers in the context of disabled people (Shaw & Coles, 2004; Shaw, Veitch, & Coles, 2005). And while recent research has re-engaged with definitional issues of social tourism (Minnaert et al., 2007) and of the impacts of social tourism interventions on health and social policy connections (McCabe, 2009; Minnaert, Maitland, & Miller, 2009) overall, this tends to come from a benefits perspective leaving little analysis of the systems and structures of the supply of social tourism. Recent research has addressed some of these gaps that highlighted significant systemic and structural differences (Diekmann et al., 2009 aforementioned). It is therefore critical to understand how the EU has shifted its 'orientation' towards social tourism in order to evaluate the organisation and supply of services in this sector of the industry.

The European Commission understanding of social tourism

The concept of social tourism has its origins firmly in the social democratic ideal for a fair and just society, where equality of access to leisure travel is encouraged because of its benefits to individuals and families. The EC became interested in social tourism issues in this context and focused its efforts on the different concepts of social tourism and compared the levels of funding in the different countries (Commission des Communautés Européennes – D.G. XXIII – Unité Tourisme, 1994). In 2002, the 'European Economic and Social Committee on Social tourism in Europe' states in its opinion (2002 – article 2.2.2):

> ...starting from the premise that tourism is a general right which we should try to make accessible to everyone we can say that an activity constitutes social tourism whenever three conditions are met
> – Real-life circumstances are such that it is totally or partially impossible to fully exercise the right to tourism. This may be due to economic conditions, physical or mental disability, personal or family isolation, reduced mobility, geographical difficulties, and a wide variety of causes which ultimately constitute a real obstacle.
> – Someone – be it a public or private institution, a company, a trade union, or simply an organised group of people – decides to take action to overcome or reduce the obstacle which prevents a person from exercising their right to tourism.
> – This action is effective and actually helps a group of people to participate in tourism in a manner which respects the values of sustainability, accessibility and solidarity.

In 2006, the Commissioner for Enterprise and Industry presented the 'Renewed Tourism Policy' (COM, 2006) focusing broadly on the economic growth aspects of tourism as an industry. In that report, the Commission acknowledged the crucial role of tourism in the EU economy, recognising also the need for sustainable growth, which balances job creation with the promotion of social and environmental objectives. The Renewed Tourism Policy was followed in 2007 with the launch of the TSG report

'Action for more sustainable European tourism', emphasising specifically three major aims: (1) Economic prosperity; (2) Social equity and cohesion; (3) Environmental and cultural protection (Tourism Sustainability Group, 2007, p. 3). Although social tourism was already on the EU agenda, the second aim does not refer specifically to social tourism, but with respect to either: the enhancement of socio-cultural life of host communities and their involvement in tourism development in their region; or to provide a safe or fulfilling experience for all visitors without discrimination.

Simultaneously however, between 2006 and 2009 the Tourism Unit organised (in collaboration with ISTO) three conferences on social tourism issues. The first conference in 2006 was themed: 'Tourism for all: State of the play and existing practices in the EU'. For the EU, the concept of TFA is an aim for social cohesion in European societies. According to the Commission's interpretation of the diversity of the 'Tourism for all' agenda, social tourism constitutes a great potential market, which deserves to be developed and encouraged. Social tourism is considered as an economic response to congestion and seasonality problems and in that ideal, lays the foundation for the current Calypso project.

The second conference took place within the context of the 'European Year of Equal Opportunities for All: 2007'. This initiative was based on the Lisbon strategy. This strategy developed first by the EU in 2000 focused among other issues on increasing the competiveness of services and aimed for the creation of 'more and better jobs through the sustainable growth of tourism in Europe and globally' (COM, 2006, p. 4). According to the EC website: 'the main objective of the workshop for stakeholders on senior citizens and youths was to identify whether there exists the possibility of extending collaboration on social tourism in different Member States that are currently less active than others in this field' (http://ec. europa.eu/enterprise/tourism). The last conference in 2008 was again based on the Lisbon strategy analysing social Tourism in the EU: Youths and Senior Citizens. In 2008, social tourism stakeholders expressed the wish to initiate procedures leading to the establishment of a tourism pilot project for senior citizens that could assist in the improvement of seasonality problems of the tourism sector which precipitated the Calypso study. Thus, the activities of the EC illustrate a significant shift in orientation towards economic position on social tourism which is far removed from the earlier focus on social tourism as workers right and for individual and social benefits, exemplified by the following quote:

> In promoting access for groups for which going on holiday has progressively become more difficult, social tourism strengthens the tourism industry's revenue generation potential. Social tourism aids mobility and enables off-season tourism to be developed, particularly in regions where tourism is highly seasonal. Accordingly, social tourism encourages the creation of longer-lasting employment opportunities in the tourism sector, in line with the Lisbon Strategy, by making it possible to extend such jobs beyond the respective peak season.
> (http://ec.europa.eu/enterprise/tourism/major_activities/social_tourism/index_en.htm) June 2009

This reorientation of policies on social tourism perhaps belies a broader political hegemonic shift in favour of neo-liberalism and policies that favour the individual rather than society as seen across wider policy contexts. The shift serves as both an enabler – encouraging private sector engagement in social tourism – while also exacerbating the problem of lack of clarity concerning what social tourism stands for and thus a common European approach.

Social tourism systems in Europe

Three major elements have to be taken into account for the analysis of social tourism systems: funding, target groups and facilities. While in some countries, the social tourism sector is entirely supported by unions and specific social tourism organisations (e.g. France), in other countries, social tourism activity relies totally on the commercial tourism sector and yet others, entirely on the third sector. Many countries have a mixed system. Social tourism depends in many countries on public funding and consequently on specific national policies requiring the political backing of social tourism as a welfare policy tool. The political approach is critical in determining individual national responses. For instance, while in Romania holiday vouchers have been introduced towards the end of 2008, they have been abandoned in Austria (Diekmann et al., 2009). In the UK, social tourism policies are exclusively supported by the charity sector addressing specific target groups in a mostly unconnected way, in France and Belgium social tourism addresses all layers of society and is publicly funded. In Germany, the situation is different again, partially due to the historical background on the one hand of the programme 'Strength through joy (Kraft durch Freude – KdF)', and on the other hand by the integration of the people of the former socialist regime in Eastern Germany.

There are three major social tourism implementation schemes that can be identified throughout Europe, however each country often includes two or more combinations, high-lighting very clearly the difficulty in the comparison of social tourism issues. In some countries, the use of holiday vouchers provides the consumer with a possibility of choosing commercial tourism accommodation (e.g. Hungary, Romania), while in others the holiday voucher is a tool of providing access to a social tourism facility (e.g. France) (Diekmann et al., 2009, p. 28). A more detailed analysis of the three elements confirms the difficulty in finding a European consensus of social tourism.

Funding

Two major types of funding can be observed: either infrastructure-orientated funding or ben-eficiary-orientated funding. The major distinction is between direct and indirect state funding with one exception being the UK. Here, social tourism is primarily organised by the third sector by charities such as the Family Holiday Association, the Family Fund (a provider of aid for families and particularly for disabled children), the Youth Hostel Association (YHA), the trade union Unison Welfare and literally hundreds more providing respite care and/or breaks. The intervention of these organisations is very often small scale, regional and largely they do not identify themselves as social tourism providers, rather as providers of respite care services. This activity can attract government funding, through local govern-ment or through targeted programmes such as in respect of dementia and terminal illness. Only in 2007, the UK formalised their collaboration with the Social Tourism Declaration. The Family Holiday Association has very good relationships with the travel industry, which gives them access to discounted or even free holidays. This charity receives the majority of its funding via individual donations, the tourism industry and income from trusts or through events.

While in other countries social tourism is funded directly through the state (or region). This is delivered through a ministry grant either directly to beneficiaries or to suppliers. In terms of indirect funding, the state subsidises unions or health and welfare organisations. For instance, in Germany, social tourism is funded by the social ministry of the 'Länder' (regions). This ministry distributes finance through a lead organisation (Bundesarbeitsgemeinschaft Familie-nerholung (BAGFE)) to various sub-organisations, often holiday centres. In Romania, funding comes from two sources. The funding of a special offer (discounts and special prices) aimed mainly at people living on low incomes. The funding comes through the national budget via the National House of Pensions and Health Insurances (CNPAS). Prices accepted during

CNPAS's auctions are covered partly by the client and partly by the CNPAS: clients pay only part of the price, calculated according to their income (pension or wage). However, a lack of funding recently halted the construction of new social tourism facilities and induced reflection on the possibility of introducing a holiday voucher system such as in France (Diekmann et al., 2009, p. 30).

In Poland, social tourism after having played an important role under socialist regime, has declined and now refers mostly to children and youth tourism. Funding is provided directly through ministerial budgets, highlighting effectiveness issues. A particularity of Poland is a law that procures a preferential 7% VAT for the organisation of children's or youth tourist trips (whether the trip is commercial or not) (Diekmann et al., 2009, p. 30). A ministerial programme for the development of children's and the youth's tourism in Poland up to 2011 has recently been established.

In Belgium, France and Spain, the systems of support are quite advanced and well organised. Social tourism in Belgium is financed directly through the regional governments, but also indirectly through unions and health and welfare organisations providing social tourism facilities. The situation is similar in France, though the system is mainly based on holiday vouchers which are linked to workers unions. In Spain, the most important social tourism programme is partly financed by IMSERSO, the Institute of Senior and Social Services depending on the Labour and social Affairs Ministry. IMSERSO finance 30% while the user pays 70% for different holiday programmes consisting in taking senior citizens to commercial tourism facilities (Diekmann et al., 2009).

Target groups

Social tourism is widely linked to issues, such as social exclusion, non-participation, accessibility and governance although not exclusively linked to a poverty perspective. Thus, social tourism not only seeks to address economically disadvantaged people but aims to address a whole range of societal phenomenon affecting different groups in society such as single parents, seniors, youth and disabled, etc. The target groups of the social tourism activity have increased a great deal due to changes in leisure behaviour, expectations and the general shift in values that focuses on consumption experiences as opposed to material goods. Along with demographic changes, this is also due to an increased accessibility of cheap commercial tourism to groups which would otherwise require social assistance and the need to address newly emergent target groups for social tourism initiatives (Diekmann et al., 2009, p. 27).

The main target groups are represented in all European countries, although the relative distribution might differ among them. Due to historical and political reasons, two major segments can be distinguished: working people and unemployed people. While the first group benefits from social tourism through their unions or employers in countries like in France and Belgium, the second group benefits mainly via direct state-backed schemes. The target group analysis is directly linked to sources of funding either direct or indirect through public health care, workers unions or charities. It should also be stressed that there is sometimes a difference between target groups and the actual consumer groups of social tourism. Direct state funding, for example, is most often channelled through NGOs or charities, which deal with the needs of specific target groups or supply the facilities. The British Government provides a direct grant to the YHA (England and Wales) to subsidise summer activity camps for children from disadvantaged backgrounds for instance. Most of the countries listed also have NGOs and/or charity systems targeting different target groups according to areas of priority need.

In Germany, social tourism funding is mainly targeted at families, including single parent families, adoptive and carer families, or grand-parents caring for children. In most Länder, one child is enough to benefit from funding, but in some, two or more children are a condition for receiving the funding. Families generally stay in Germany or in two foreign countries, which have family centres (France and Hungary). The aim is to foster exchange and experiences with other families, and to repair and restore family relationships, which are vulnerable to breakdown (Bundesarbeitsgemeinschaft Familienerholung [BAGFE], 2009). The conditions are similar for disadvantaged families in UK who can, for instance, through the support of social workers apply for a holiday with the Family Holiday Association. Poland focuses mainly on youth and children holiday programmes, while Spain concentrates mainly on seniors through the IMSERSO programme. The main underlying social policy area here is to encourage social participation among groups that are seen as vulnerable to isolation or in the case of youth travel, to broaden horizons and create opportunities for new experiences. Belgium and France consider themselves to have a broad-ranged approach driven by social cohesion goals (see for example UNAT, 2006). But taking a closer look, it is mainly the working middleclass who are the principal users of social tourism facilities, which appears to arise as a consequence of the facilities belonging either to worker unions or to the public health care organisations (Caire, 2007).

Supply and facilities

In terms of the supply of social tourism services, there are different types addressing different market segments. For instance, in France, Chauvin (2002) listed six different types of 'tourist products' managed by either union, social health care or religious organisations:

- Holiday villages for families and groups.
- Sport and youth accommodation, mainly youth hostels.
- Holiday centres for children and youngsters.
- School trips.
- Language trips.
- Trips for adults in another country.

However, social tourism in Germany is in the hands of the BAGFE that comprises three different organisations (two confessional (catholic and protestant) and the other secular). Altogether they provide about 130 family centres throughout Germany. The organisations distinguish themselves from commercial suppliers because their main aim is not profit, but family-orientated welfare as a core element of all policies and activities. On the contrary to Germany, in Belgium, the unions are the owners of many social tourism facilities. The purpose for their involvement in the provision of accommodation facilities is comparable to the German case, to provide an opportunity for social exchange with other people. There are also very different points of view on the services provided by social tourism. In Romania, for instance, social tourism focuses on three basic services: accommodation, meals and medical care in spas. While in Belgium, infrastructures of social tourism, in particular for youth tourism, provide additional services and activities (guided tours, parties, etc.). In the UK, the provision of funding for activity/adventure holidays for young people is comparable. Common issues in terms of the supply of facilities seem to be the constant quest for quality improvement in social tourism facilities in order to meet the needs of more demanding clients and sustain competition with commercial infrastructures (Diekmann et al., 2009, p. 29).

How social is social tourism?

As demonstrated, the different systems have varying levels of links with the 'commercial tourism', mainstream tourism sector. Maurin (2004) distinguishes social tourism from commercial tourism by highlighting the focus on target groups for intervention and community development aspects of the social tourism sector. This is in contrast to the commercial sector where the focus on profit and the creation of market segments foster an inner-directed perspective, in terms of the firm and its operations and position in the market. However, links do exist and are complex in many countries, there are often overlapping commercial and social tourism activities. It is possible to suggest that the links between the social and commercial tourism sectors may give an indication on 'how' 'social' the social tourism provision in each country is in reality.

In the UK, beneficiaries of charity programmes are often also supported by the mainstream industry through discounted package deals, subsidised transport or commercial tourism accommodation provision. In Spain, the aim of the social tourism programme IMSERSO is notably to help the commercial tourism sector overcome poor low-season occupancy levels in the mass tourism resorts. In France and Belgium, instead of using commercial accommodation, social tourism facilities are accessible to everybody, including a non-specific 'social tourism' market, for their main aim is to foster social cohesion between social groups. The consequence however is that the holiday centres compete more and more with commercial tourism facilities. In the UK, the YHA is a classic case of a charity and commercial operation. In recent years, it has seen its market in the budget accommodation sector being targeted by the budget hotel sector, leaving it to compete on a commercial basis and to step-up its focus on the subsidised 'social tourism' market.

Figure 1 highlights the extent that systems for social tourism are actually inclusive in terms of representing the 'tourism for all' philosophy. It shows that the countries with the most developed social tourism system can actually be argued to be less inclusive than they could be for unemployed and other marginalised members of society who remain excluded by the state-backed, unionised holiday voucher. That this is the case in countries with a 'social tourism culture' is very probably linked to the origins of social tourism after WW2 as labour (union) organisations. In that sense, social tourism in France, for instance, is very well developed, but perhaps fails to reach the most in need of support and fails to adapt to new forms of poverty and social exclusion (as identified by McCabe, 2009, Cass, Shove, & Urry, 2005 for example). Figure 1 also stresses the fact that indirect state-backed schemes tend to be more commercial in orientation than those with direct state aid/facilities. In some circumstances, where the aim of social tourism schemes is to integrate the sector with the mainstream commercial sector to achieve true social equity, there is a risk of excluding some target groups, both on financial grounds (the accommodation is too expensive) and more importantly in social terms, feeling uncomfortable or awkward, mixing with social groups outside their norms. While Minnaert et al. (2009) argue that the benefits of increasing access to holidays can lead to increases in social and human capital, care needs to be taken to ensure that social tourists feel the benefits without any undue pressures in terms of integration or community cohesion.

Caire (2007) suggests that visitors to social tourism accommodation contained a large number of people who are employed with better working conditions than in general in the commercial tourism sector. This was also the case in the UK with the YHA membership being predominantly middle class (McCabe, 2005). While in France, around 1530 centres (UNAT, 2004) host tourists from all groups of society, in Germany for instance, the 180 (BAGFE, 2009) social tourism accommodation structures receive mainly families

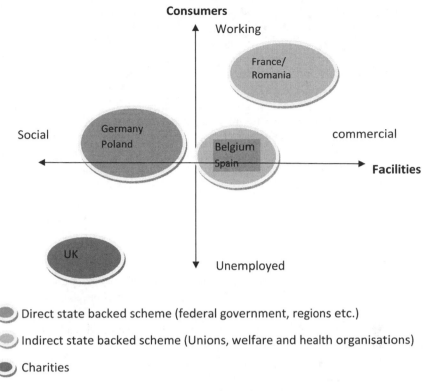

Figure 1.   How social is social tourism – accessibility to social tourism?

who could not afford commercial holidays. It is clear that there are real differences in the ways in which social tourism opportunities are orientated towards specific target groups which could indicate a cultural or social attitude either positive or negative towards social tourism centres or accommodation units by 'mainstream' (i.e. commercial) tourists. The cultural attitudes surrounding social forms of tourism may be linked to the different meanings of the term in different countries.

Conclusions

This comparative analysis of social tourism in a selection of EU countries has highlighted the major constraints towards the development of a common approach to social tourism within the EU. However, some key themes have emerged which could be used as building blocks towards this goal. Social tourism, although having been borne out of an era domi-nated by social ideals and the workers movement, has elided into a policy framework driven by neoliberal social democratic principles. Thus, social tourism in Europe seems to represent an awkward mix of social liberalism and the concerns for propping up an important sector of the European economy (the mainstream tourism industry). The twin issues do not necessarily need to be mutually exclusive. For social tourism to work, there needs to be: a focus on defining the social function/purpose and goals underpinning the action (including the identification of the benefits for supporting social tourism); the implementation of a system to achieve the goals; the identification of target groups for the actions; the allocation of targeted funds to meet the objectives, as well as a system to deliver funds (i.e. through NGOs or third party organisations); an understanding of the roles of the different bodies in coordinating and delivering the actions, including the role of the private sector; and finally a sound system for communicating the goals and steps in the actions to all parties concerned. This last point seems to be particularly important considering the lack of awareness about and the rationale for implementing social tourism in many EU countries.

There is scope for difference within individual countries both in terms of the target groups but there must be a social purpose underlying the intervention. There is a very real danger that the commercialisation of social tourism could lead to further exclusionary practice with some target groups being isolated from participation. Furthermore, there must be an understanding of how the target groups will benefit from the actions in order to evaluate the success of any programme. It is apparent that the present intervention in social tourism by the EU could be further developed to identify common issues within a framework such as that proposed here to increase the chances for flexibility, integration and successful implementation.

The overview provided in this comparison between a few European countries has revealed the great variety of social tourism concepts and systems in the EU and highlighted a number of issues to take forward into further research and in terms of policy development. These differences were not only in terms of the political and policy orientations towards the funding of social tourism structures but also in the delivery of services, the supply of facilities and the prioritisation of different target groups, and critically the links between the social and commercial tourism sectors. In some cases there is little difference between social and commercial tourism where benefits do not seem to reach target groups. In others, there are less integrated structures but in these cases, provision is well targeted and is able to meet the needs of specific disadvantaged groups.

Just as social tourism developed differently in each country alongside the cultural conventions and political histories, its relationship or level of integration into the commercial tourism sector has similarly evolved. The EU has reshaped its policy orientation to social tourism, from an ideology of social justice, towards a more industry-focused, pragmatic view, positioning social tourism as sustainable tourism and vital to a dynamic and ever-more important plank of the EU economy. There is a pressing need for further research on best practices, a common framework for the evaluation of social tourism initiatives and research on the economic impact of social tourism on the tourism economy.

The ideal of the EU to implement a common social tourism framework seems illusive. It is questionable whether social tourists benefit from cross-cultural interaction (particularly considering the vast array of target groups and their needs). The comparison of different countries showed that there is little basis at present for a single 'social tourism in Europe'. Yet, to judge which system is the most suitable is extremely difficult since national systems and conceptions of social tourism are closely linked to each country's history, political and institutional organisation. Furthermore, one common point is the decreasing availability of public funding for social welfare. In that sense, the interest of the EU in social tourism is of major importance, but it is questionable whether a distinction between social and commercial tourism sector can be identified when the supply side is mainly part of the commercial sector except in France and Belgium.

Evidence suggests that before trying to collaborate towards a common framework for social tourism, comparative research is needed to identify the main issues. However, the opportunity for this was overlooked and instead in 2008, a new TSG was initiated with an increased focus on social tourism. Calypso funded a study for an implementation scheme for social tourism in Europe aiming at lowering (among others) seasonality of employment in the accommodation sector. However, the diversity of social tourism systems and consequent issues represents a major challenge for the EC in creating links and the development of a common policy. In many ways, the EU's approach with Calypso pre-empts much needed research on the fundamental differences between systems and schemes so that policy and academic debate can both be developed in an integrated and coherent way. In this way, we will be much further towards a better understanding of what works best, for whom, and in which ways. Not only that, but in terms of influencing national and regional policy in the larger EU, greater strength of research findings would provide an enhanced lever for an integrated policy, providing greater benefits for greater numbers of social tourists and increasing the sustainability of the tourism economy of Europe.

Notes

1. International Organisation of Social Tourism.
2. Union Nationale des Associations de Tourisme.
3. Family Holiday Association.

References

Abdel-Ghaffar, A., Handy, M., Jafari, J., Kreul, L., & Stivala, F. (1992). Conference reports: Youth tourism. *Annals of Tourism Research, 19*(4), 792–795.

Bundesarbeitsgemeinschaft Familienerholung. (2009, July). Retrieved from http://www.urlaub-mit-der-familie.de/start/index.php.

BITS (1996). *Montreal declaration: For a humanistic and social vision of tourism.* Retrieved from http://www.bits.org.

Caire G. (2005). Le Tiers secteur, une troisième voie vers le développement durable? L'exemple des ambitions et des difficultés d'un autre tourisme. In Concepts of the third sector: The European debate, ISTR, EMES, 27–29 April 2005.

Caire G. (2006). Les associations françaises de tourisme social face aux politiques européennes, Document de travail, *Recherche sur l'industrie et l'innovation*. Retrieved from http://riifr.univ-littoral.fr/wp-content/uploads/2007/01/CaireDT40.pdf.

Caire, G. (2007). Les associations françaises de tourisme: De l'impulsion d'un marché de masse aux difficultés d'un « autre » tourisme. In A. Dussuet & J.M. Lauzanas (Eds.), *L'économie sociale entre informel et formel: Paradoxes et innovations* (pp. 129–150). Rennes: Presses Universitaires.

Cass, N., Shove, E., & Urry, J. (2005). Social exclusion, mobility and access. *The Sociological Review, 53,* 539–555.

Chauvin, J. (2002). *Le tourisme social et associations en France: Acteur majeur de l'économie sociale.* Paris, France: Editions L'Harmattan.

COM. (2006). 'Renewed Tourism Policy' 134 final of 17.03.2006.

Commission des Communautés Européennes – D.G. XXIII – Unité Tourisme. (1994). *Les différentes notions du tourisme social: L'évolution de l'offre et de la demande.* Luxemburg: UNIPUB, Management Conseil Communication.

Couveia, A. (1995). Identité et encadrement international du tourisme social, Seminarion Internacional de Turismo Social, Calvià (Mallorca).

Diekmann, A., Duquesne, A.-M., Maulet, G., & De Nicolo, B. (2009). *Employment in the European Social Tourism Sector.* Brussels: Report for EFFAT and BITS, LIToTeS (ULB).

Graburn, N.H. (1983). Editorial comment. *Annals of Tourism Research, 10,* 1–3

Hall, D., & Brown, F. (1996). Towards welfare focus for tourism research. *Progress in Tourism and Hospitality Research, 2*(1), 41–57.

Hall, D., & Brown, F. (2006). *Tourism and welfare: Ethics, responsibility and sustainable well-being.* Wallingford: CABI.

Hazel, N. (2005). Holidays for children and families in need: An exploration of the research and policy context for social tourism in the UK. *Children and Society, 19,* 225–236.

Haulot, A. (1982). Social tourism: Current dimensions of future developments. *Journal of Travel Research, 20,* 40.

Higgins-Desbiolles, F. (2006). More than an 'industry': The forgotten power of tourism as a social force. *Tourism Management, 27*(6), 1192–1208.

Hunter-Jones, P. (2004). Young people, holiday taking and cancer: An exploratory analysis. *Tourism Management, 25,* 249–258.

Hunziker, W. (1957). Cio che rimarrebbe ancora da dire sul turismo sociale. *Revue de tourisme, 2,* 52–57.

Jefferson, A. (1991). Demographics, youth and tourism. *Tourism Management, 12*(1), 73–75.

Krippendorf, J. (1987). *The holiday makers: Understanding the impact of leisure and travel.* London, UK: William Heinemann.

La Documentation Française. (1992). *Le Tourisme social et familial.* Paris: la documentation française.

Maurin, E. (2004). *Le ghetto français. Enquête sur le séparatisme social.* Paris: Author.

McCabe, S. (2005). *National User Survey. Unpublished Report for the Youth Hostel Association (England and Wales).* Matlock, Derbyshire: YHA.

McCabe, S. (2009). Who needs a holiday? Evaluating social tourism. *Annals of Tourism Research, 36*(4), 667–688.

Minnaert, L., Maitland, R., & Miller, G. (2007). Social tourism and its ethical foundations. *Tourism Culture and Communication, 7,* 7–17.

Minnaert, L., Maitland, R., & Miller, G. (2009). Tourism and social policy: The value of social tourism. *Annals of Tourism Research, 36*(2), 316–334.

Mundt, J. (2004). *Tourismuspolitik.* München: Oldenburg Wissenschaftsverlag.

Richards, G. (1998). Time for a Holiday? Social rights and international tourism consumption. *Time and Society, 7*(1), 145–160.

Richards, G. (1999). Vacations and the quality of life: Patterns and structures. *Journal of Business Research, 44,* 189–198.

Shaw, G., & Coles, T. (2004). Disability, holidaymaking and the tourism industry in the UK. *Tourism Management, 25,* 397–403.

Shaw, G., Veitch, C., & Coles, T. (2005). Access, disability and tourism. *Review International, 8,* 167–177.

Tourism Sustainability Group. (2007, February). *Action for more sustainable European tourism: Report of the Tourism Sustainability Group.* February 2007, European Commission, 47.

UNAT. (2004, October). *L'apport social du tourisme associatif dans les territoires. Etude réalisée pour le conseil national du tourisme dans le cadre de la session « droit aux vacances».* Retrieved from http://www.unat.asso.fr.

UNAT. (2006). *Un tourisme associatif: Une réalité économique.* Retrieved from http://www.unat. asso.fr.

Towards a 'tourism for all' policy for Ireland: achieving real sustainability in Irish tourism

Kevin Griffin and Jane Stacey

School of Hospitality Management and Tourism, Dublin Institute of Technology, Cathal Brugha Street, Dublin 1, Ireland

The importance of tourism for all initiatives in contributing to the economic and social well-being of citizens has long been recognised by many European Union Member States. The European Commission and the European Economic and Social Committee have acknowledged not only the social value of tourism for all in terms of personal development, well-being and social cohesion, but also its potential economic value in terms of revenue generation, job creation and regional development.

This paper focuses on Ireland, where the concept of tourism for all is poorly understood. While social inclusion is explicitly on the national policy agenda, Irish tourism has tended to be viewed entirely through economic lenses, with little acknowledgement of its social value. Within the context of sustainable development, which is a stated policy objective in Ireland, environmental issues have received a disproportionate level of attention within the tourism domain. The core argument forwarded here is that unless Irish tourism policy-makers turn their attention to 'making holidays available for all', Irish tourism will fail to meet at least one of the eight key tourism sustainability challenges, as identified by the European Commission (2007) and further fail to realise the existing Irish policy commitment to sustainable tourism development.

Introduction

'Tourism for All' 'involves the extension of the benefits of holidays to economically marginal groups, such as the unemployed, single-parent families, pensioners and the handicapped' (Hall, 2005, p. 152). The importance of tourism in contributing to economic and social well-being has long been recognised by many European Union Member States. The European Commission and the European Economic and Social Committee (EESC) have acknowledged not only the social value of tourism for all in terms of personal development, well-being and social cohesion, but also its potential economic value in terms of revenue generation, job creation and regional development.

This paper focuses on Ireland, where in contrast to many European countries, the concept of tourism for all is poorly understood. Despite rapid economic advances in Ireland during the 1990's and early 2000's, tackling poverty and social exclusion remains a challenge. Social inclusion, well-being and quality of life are firmly on the Irish policy agenda, being key pillars of the National Development Plan 2007–2013 (Government of Ireland, 2007) and the National Action Plan For Social Inclusion 2007–2016 (Office for Social Inclusion, 2007). Tourism, however, is an exception, as it is often viewed entirely through economic lenses, with little acknowledgement or recognition of its social value.

Holidaying is now a standard lifestyle practice for a majority of Irish citizens, yet EU Survey on Income and Living Conditions (SILC) data show that while Ireland enjoyed economic prosperity, almost a quarter of Irish citizens could not afford to take an annual holiday for financial reasons (Central Statistics Office, 2007), with this proportion rising to almost a third in recent times (Central Statistics Office, 2009). Unless Irish tourism policy-makers turn their attention to 'making holidays available to all', then Irish tourism will fail to meet at least one of the eight key tourism sustainability challenges identified by the European Commission (2007).

This paper begins by conceptualising tourism for all from a range of perspectives. The recognition which the concept receives at European level is examined, and tourism for all is situated within a sustainability framework. The absence of an official Irish policy on the topic is considered. The core section of the paper follows – an examination of the challenges which need to be tackled before Ireland can develop an official tourism for all policy. The paper concludes with observations on the development of an Irish policy in this regard.

Conceptualising 'tourism for all' and 'holidaying'

Hall defines social tourism as 'the relationships and phenomena in the field of tourism resulting from participation in travel by economically weak or otherwise disadvantaged elements in society' (Hall, 2005, p. 141). Meanwhile, the EESC refers to measures 'designed to make travel accessible to the highest number of people, particularly the most underprivileged sectors of the population' (European Economic and Social Committee [EESC], 2006, p. 3). While definitions that interrogate the concept tourism for all (or 'social tourism' as it is commonly referred to in those countries with the strongest traditions of the practice) vary, the underlying philosophy is that tourism and holidaying should be accessible to all, without discrimination and should be practiced in a manner that is linked to sustainable development (Jolin, 2004).

Holidaying has become a widespread social practice in advanced economies, as economic prosperity has led to leisure being regarded as an essential part of individual and community well-being (Dawson, 1988). Additionally, there is an underlying assumption that leisure practices such as holidays are beneficial in many ways (Hobson & Dietrich, 1994 cited in Gilbert & Abdullah, 2002). Holiday-taking is generally viewed as a mentally and physically healthy pursuit that increases quality of life.

A number of empirical studies in recent years have specifically focused on the benefits of holidays to those from disadvantaged backgrounds (see English Tourist Board, 1976; Ghate & Hazel, 2002; Gilbert & Abdullah, 2002; Lewis, 2001; Wigfall, 2004; Minnaert, Maitland, & Miller, 2009; Quinn & Stacey, 2010; Smith & Hughes, 1999; Voysey, 2000). These studies provide evidence for the existence of real benefits, including:

- an essential break from (often stressful) routine and home environment;
- opportunities for social mixing and interaction with new people;
- increased life satisfaction;

- subjective well-being and enhanced quality of life;
- improved mental and physical health and well-being;
- opportunities for personal development through new experiences in new environments;
- improved self-image and self-esteem;
- refreshment and improvement of relationships;
- establishing feelings of normalcy.

The benefits of holidays identified above are also reflective of the general holiday benefits identified in general tourism literature (e.g. Cohen & Taylor, 1992; Mannell & Iso-Ahola, 1987).

There is also evidence, albeit limited, suggesting broader benefits, impacting on individual and family well-being (Brimacombe, 2003; Gilbert & Abdullah, 2002; Smith & Hughes, 1999; Wigfall, 2004), contributing financial and social benefits for society in general (Corlyon & La Placa, 2006; Hazel, 2005; Hughes, 1991).

Holidaying non-participation and social exclusion

However, holidaying is a socially exclusionist activity. While holidaying has become an important social phenomenon (European Economic and Social Committee [EESC], 2003), participation is by no means universal (Shaw & Williams, 2002). An important implication here is that as holidays are now a significant part of contemporary life, exclusion from participation may be an indicator of poverty (Hughes, 1991; Smith & Hughes, 1999) as it suggests an inability to participate in the commonly accepted style of life of the community (Dawson, 1988). Economic constraints are the single most important factor responsible for involuntary non-participation in holidaying (English Tourist Board, 1985; Eurobarometer, 1998; European Commission, 2001; Haukeland, 1990; Hughes, 1991; Jolin, 2004). Other constraining factors include: illness and disability (physiological and psychological); mobility and access; family circumstances; caring for dependants; and problems associated with ageing. Many of these other constraining factors overlap with the economic variable in producing social marginality and exclusion (English Tourist Board, 1989; Seaton, 1992; Shaw & Williams, 2002; Temowetsky, 1983; Van Raaji & Francken, 1984).

The benefits identified above provide support for Hughes (1991, p. 196) who concluded that:

> if there are real benefits to be derived from a holiday (especially for the disadvantaged), and a holiday is a 'necessity', there may well be a good case for active financial intervention in order to bring holidays within reach of such deprived persons.

Meanwhile, Smith (1998) claims that the benefits of holidays are similar to the benefits put forward in favour of increasing access to sport and leisure activities on behalf of disadvantaged groups. If these two arguments are considered, there would appear to be a legitimate argument for tackling the factors that limit participation, and thus including access to holiday-taking in national policy.

Tourism for all policy perspectives

Internationally, governments of different political persuasions have justified the incorporation of leisure into social policy on the basis of both the benefits accruing to individuals and society as a whole. Haulot (1981, p. 212) argues that: 'social tourism ... finds justification in that its individual and collective objectives are consistent with the view that all measures taken by modern society should ensure more justice, more dignity and improved enjoyment of life for all citizens' (as cited in Hall, 2005, p. 152). Accordingly, access to holidaying opportunities has been dominated by three inter-related but distinct social rationales:

- Tourism as a social right, as evidenced by various international declarations, dating back to at least 1948 when the Universal Declaration of Human Rights underscored that 'every one has the right to rest and leisure' (United Nations, 1948, Art. 24).
- Tourism as contributing to social welfare, with implications for individual and collective well-being (Haukeland, 1990).
- Tourism as contributing to social inclusion, fighting against inequality and exclusion and supporting social cohesion (Jolin, 2004).

Recognition for the concept arises not solely from a social but also from an economic perspective – tourism for all has been promoted as a means of economic growth, job creation, regional development and addressing the issue of seasonality.

In many European countries, there is well-established government acknowledgement for the importance of holidaying. Direct government support for annual holiday taking is provided, either as a subsidy to the consumer or the provider. However, there is no one form of tourism for all provision common across Europe or indeed within individual countries. The plurality of expression of tourism for all reflects these varying ideological and social attitudes (Richards, 1992, as cited in Smith, 1998; Lanquar, 1996).

Tourism for all at European level

The European Union has acknowledged not only the social value of tourism for all in terms of personal development, well-being and social cohesion, but also its potential economic value in terms of revenue generation, job creation and regional development.

Research conducted under the Belgian Presidency of the European Union in 2001 high-lighted a broad variation in the then 15 Member States, with countries such as France, Belgium and Italy possessing developed policies while others, such as Ireland and the United Kingdom, were found to be lagging behind in State engagement. A European Ministerial Conference on the issue proposed that each Member State should identify its own policies and procedures.

The EESC subsequently called for the establishment of tourism for all programmes in all EU Member States, 'making them financially accessible to everyone and conducive to the well-being of users, providing workers with all-year-round employment and underpinning the profitability of companies' (European Economic and Social Committee [EESC], 2003, p. 13). More recently, the EESC (2006, p. 68) underscored its commitment to tourism for all, stating that:

> Everyone has the right to rest on a daily, weekly and yearly basis, and the right to the leisure time that enables them to develop every aspect of their personality and their social integration. Clearly, everyone is entitled to exercise this right to personal development. The right to tourism is a concrete expression of this general right, and social tourism is underpinned by the desire to ensure that it is universally accessible in practice.

While discussing the concept of tourism for all, this opinion document links itself to the right to participate in tourism as enshrined in Article 7 of the United Nations World Tourism Organisation's, 1999 Global Code of Ethics for Tourism (EESC, 2006: Section 2.1).

Recent developments at European Commission level have focused on economic and social aspects within the context of the Lisbon Strategy, with the current Calypso programme specifically focused on 'enhancing employment, extending the seasonality spread, strengthening European citizenship and improving regional/local economies through the development of social tourism' (European Commission, 2009, p. 1).

The Calypso programme seeks to identify and disseminate information on existing best practice while ensuring accessibility to tourism for different target groups and thereby involve additional strata of the European population in tourism. The Commission highlights the following benefits of tourism for all:

- generating economic activity and growth across Europe;
- improving tourism seasonality patterns across Europe;
- create more and better jobs in the tourism sector;
- increase the European citizenship of target groups (youths, seniors, people with disabilities and families facing difficult social circumstances) (European Commission, 2009).

These benefits overlap quite closely with the challenges of sustainable tourism discussed in the following section.

Contextualising 'tourism for all' within a sustainability framework

Over the last 20 years, the concept of sustainable tourism development has become almost universally accepted as a desirable approach to tourism development (Sharpley, 2003), achieving 'virtual global endorsement as the new [tourism] industry paradigm' (Godfrey, 1996, p. 60). Defined by the United Nations World Tourism Organisation (2004) as tourism which 'meets the needs of present tourists and host regions, while protecting and enhancing opportunities for the future', it refers in its core, to a blending of environmental, economic and socio-cultural aspects of tourism, seeking to ensure that a suitable balance is established between these three dimensions.

Tourism for all sits comfortably within this concept, since truly sustainable tourism can include socially motivated practices to make holidays accessible for all. In addition, it spreads tourism spatially and temporally, educating and integrating the society. While traditionally, the development of a policy on tourism for all would have focused on benefits such as inter-cultural understanding and tolerance, there is a growing literature which suggests that viable economic operations and thus economic benefits to all stakeholders can result from tourism for all initiatives.

Indeed, the links between tourism for all and sustainability have been recognised at the European Union level. The three key objectives of the EU Sustainable Development Strategy are: economic prosperity; social equity and cohesion; and environmental protection. In this regard, 'making holidays available to all' is explicitly identified as one of the eight key sustainability challenges facing the tourism sector (European Commission, 2007). This challenge is primarily identified on the basis of social equity and cohesion, including public health and well-being, with the challenges of physical disability and economic disadvantage specifically highlighted. 'Making holidays available to all' is also linked to the economic benefits which tourism for all may confer, helping to address two other sustainable tourism challenges, namely reducing the seasonality of demand and improving the quality of tourism jobs. Thus, the European Commission explicitly acknowledges accessibility to tourism for all EU citizens as a key sustainability issue currently facing the European tourism sector.

Eight key challenges for the tourism sector in the context of sustainability.

1. Reducing the seasonality of demand
2. Addressing the impact of tourism transport
3. Improving the quality of tourism jobs
4. Maintaining and enhancing community prosperity and quality of life, in the face of change
5. Minimising resource use and production of waste
6. Conserving and giving value to natural/cultural heritage
7. **Making holidays available for all**
8. Using tourism as a tool in global sustainable development (European Commission, 2007)

Tourism and the Irish policy context

Ireland has experienced marked social and economic change in recent decades, as might be expected in a country which enjoyed an extended period of rapid economic growth (Micklewright & Stewart, 2001). Holidaying has achieved social normalcy, yet the EU SILC (Central Statistics Office, 2007) shows that in economically prosperous times, 22 per cent of Irish citizens did not take an annual holiday for financial reasons, with this figure rising to 30 per cent more recently (Central Statistics Office, 2009).

While there is a paucity of data on the constraints to holiday taking in Ireland, available data indicate that while the incidence of holiday-taking has risen, holiday participation rates remain constrained, with the polarisation of holiday-taking mirroring the polarisation of incomes (Richards, 1998). Thus, growth in tourism numbers and revenue is due to what Richards (1998, 156) refers to as 'a concentration of consumption, rather than an extension of consumption to all social groups'. Critical commentators argue that despite economic and social change, Irish society has remained unequal (Whelan, Layte, & Maître, 2003). Tackling poverty remains a challenge and to this end, social inclusion goals are firmly on the Irish policy agenda across a breadth of domains.

The tourism domain, however, is an exception. Irish tourism policy has tended to be entirely focused on economic objectives. As the Organisation for Economic Cooperation and Development [OECD], (2004) has pointed out, tourism has grown strongly in Ireland in recent decades. While domestic tourism development and the involvement of Irish residents as tourism consumers have been priorities for decades, overall the main strategic objectives have related to wealth generation, job creation and wealth dispersion.

Since the National Sustainable Development Strategy explicitly identified a commitment to sustainable development (Department of the Environment, 1997), successive policy documents (including those within the tourism domain) have reiterated this commitment. The *New Horizons Strategy for Irish Tourism 2003–2012* outlines a vision for Irish tourism as: 'a dynamic, innovative, sustainable and highly regarded sector' (Tourism Policy Review Group, 2003, p. xiii). This pledge to sustainable tourism development is reflected in commitments by Fáilte Ireland, the National Tourism Development Authority.

However, despite this commitment, the focus has been on environmental issues, to the neglect of social challenges. It can be posited that the almost exclusively economic focus of overall Irish tourism policy, the environmental focus of 'sustainable' tourism and the related lack of consideration for tourism for all means that Irish tourism policy misses an opportunity to adhere more holistically to the principles of sustainability.

The socially exclusionist dimension to holidaying evident in Ireland has, until now, been invisible amidst wider commentaries on tourism performance. Yet, a core argument forwarded here is that unless Irish tourism policy-makers turn their attention to making holidays available to all, then Irish tourism development will fail to meet tourism targets set by the European Union, particularly the key sustainable tourism challenges identified by the European Commission (2007).

Through legislation defining increasingly shorter working weeks, institutionalising annual paid leave and establishing bank holidays, Irish citizens acquired increasing statutory rights to free time, a pre-requisite for access to leisure. In more recent decades, there is increasing acknowledgement of the State's responsibilities in promoting and facilitating access to leisure opportunities. However, to date the notion that the State might actively foster citizens' participation in holidaying for reasons relating to the innate well-being remains an alien concept in the Irish context.

Towards policy development in Ireland

It is argued in this paper that considering a tourism for all policy in Ireland would constitute an innovative response to the challenges of social exclusion and inequality, while potentially also achieving a range of economic goals. It is also suggested that such a policy would benefit from greater recognition if it were framed within the concept of sustainable tourism. However, the concept of tourism for all is virtually unrecognised in policy-making domains in Ireland, despite a history of provision in the voluntary sector that dates back to at least 80 years.

State involvement in support or provision, where it does exist, can be described as minimal, informal, *ad hoc* and uneven in its application. Furthermore, it is suggested that relevant government departments have not problematised the socially exclusionist nature of holidaying in contemporary Irish society and have yet to consider how policy thinking in the area might further social welfare, education, health or indeed economic and tourism policy goals.

Operating within a policy vacuum, the majority of the agencies facilitating access to, and provision of, holidays for those experiencing disadvantage are non-governmental organisations (NGOs) that vary in scope and scale of operations, extent of funding, organisational objectives, structures and focus. No agency (in the public, private or NGO sectors) exists solely to facilitate access to holidays, and the existing tourism for all measures are neither labelled nor recognised as such. Many agencies are involved in this activity, but all of them are simultaneously engaged in meeting broader objectives such as alleviating poverty, tackling disability or combating social exclusion. The nature and scope of the existing provision is poorly understood.

Despite the longevity of activity, the lack of awareness and recognition accorded the practice is stark. There is no official recognition that holiday provision has any valid role to play and the social value of holidaying is not part of the prevailing paradigm in Ireland. Accordingly, the authors have experienced clear challenges in promoting acceptance of the following arguments:

- that access to an annual holiday is a perceived social necessity rather than a luxury;
- that enabling access to an annual holiday can generate a series of valuable benefits at personal, inter-personal and broader societal levels, including a range of economic benefits;
- that an inability to access an annual holiday deprives people of benefits that the majority of Irish people consider to be a normal part of contemporary living and thus constitutes social exclusion, creating a series of social costs;

- that the time is now opportune for Irish policy-makers to address the area of holiday provision for those experiencing disadvantage and to bring policy and practice in line with the majority of Ireland's EU counterparts.

In suggesting that development of a tourism for all policy would be a positive move for Ireland, this paper now turns its attention to stimulating debate on policy development in the area by identifying key issues and challenges.

'Access to an annual holiday' and deprivation indicators

It would seem that a critical early step in advancing policy development is acknowledging that an inability to participate in an annual holiday constitutes a meaningful indicator of deprivation. The UK Government recognised the inability to take an annual holiday as an indicator of social exclusion in measuring child poverty in 2003 (Hazel, 2005). Irish deprivation indicators are informed by the broader EU context. At EU level, data on holidaying are gathered through the EU SILC. This survey contains a question asking: 'in the last 12 months, has your household paid for a week's holiday away from home? If no, was it because the household could not afford to or was there another reason?' This inclusion of questions about holidaying recognises the importance of access to annual holidaying as an indicator of deprivation.

In reviewing the list of deprivation indicators used in the Irish context for calculating poverty levels, 'the ability to afford a holiday away from home at least once a year' was identified for possible inclusion. However, on final analysis, it was omitted from the revised index (Maître, Nolan, & Whelan, 2006). Ironically, this was because the level of deprivation reported on this indicator equated to almost twice that reported on any other item: one in four respondents said that they lacked the financial ability to take an annual holiday. Thus, the indicator was excluded because its presence would have been unduly influential. Undoubtedly, there are political issues at play here.

However, the authors argue that what Smith (1998) refers to as the 'differential opportunity to take a holiday' is now on the brink of being problematised by Irish policy-makers. As the measurement of deprivation takes increasing cognisance of contemporary living standards and mainstream lifestyles in the context of promoting social inclusion, the validity of omitting the 'access to an annual holiday' indicator will become increasingly untenable. This argument is strengthened by reference to the EU arena, where the movement to strengthen tourism for all is gathering momentum and where, since 2008, the inability to afford a one week annual holiday away from home is one of nine indicators included in a new list of common EU deprivation indicators.

Acknowledging the value of holidaying

If policy is to be developed in this area, it is critical that knowledge about the value of holidaying is generated and disseminated. As the literature reports, a wide range of benefits is attributed to the practice of holiday-taking and the authors' findings (see Quinn & Stacey, 2010; Minnaert, Stacey, Quinn, & Griffin, 2010) attest to many of these in an Irish context. Specifically, their exploratory research found that structured, child-centred holidays broaden children's social horizons; create opportunities to learn and acquire new skills; offer exposure to positive role models and promote positive behavioural change. In addition, further benefits accrue for guardians and the wider family unit.

Generating awareness of extant tourism for all practice

Building awareness of the activities, initiatives and services currently in place throughout Ireland to facilitate access to holidaying is a prerequisite to policy development. A key finding has been that beyond those directly involved in providing and participating in the holidays, there is very little awareness of extant tourism for all activities. Undoubtedly, the task of advancing policy in the area is severely curtailed by lack of awareness.

If there is an awareness deficit evident between those agencies active in localised areas and those charged with informing and formulating decision-making in national arenas, there is a further deficit evident between agencies on the ground. NGOs are often uninformed of the activities of other NGOs; social workers and community workers only have informal and *ad hoc* links with agencies working to broaden access to holidaying; local authorities' sport and recreation services are at times entirely uncoordinated with simultaneous holiday and recreational opportunities being offered to the same cohort of children leading to timetabling clashes, etc. This lack of awareness results in a lack of coordination, integration, resource-sharing, mutual learning and networking.

Justification and rationale for policy development

This paper makes the case that facilitating access to an annual holiday for people experiencing disadvantage has value and can be justified on a number of bases. Justification for developing policy in the area can draw on a number of rationale including social welfare, economic and citizens' rights domains. It should be pointed out that in other EU countries, tourism for all interventions designed to counter exclusion on financial grounds are not targeted simply at groups within the social welfare sphere, but also at low-income individuals. Empirically, the authors' study researched both low income and social welfare-dependent families. Sometimes it appeared that the degree of social exclusion experienced by the former was the greater of the two.

Existing Irish policy statements and documents dealing with related areas provide a basis for developing a strong rationale. For example, specifically with respect to children, the *National Play Policy 2004–2008* is pertinent in that it indirectly acknowledges the value of holidaying (as a form of recreation). However, an explicit policy on broadening access to holidaying is absent. Policy development could be underpinned by a number of rationale ranging from social inclusion and a citizens' rights rationale to economic rationale. These varying viewpoints must not be conceived of as opponents but rather as integrated and complementary.

A partnership approach to policy design and delivery

It is clear that a fundamental priority of policy development in this area is to consider how public and private intervention can work in tandem with voluntary supply to address gaps in provision, improve and strengthen the existing services. To be effective, tourism for all provision must draw on the strengths of a number of partners located in public, voluntary and private sectors. Mutually beneficial ways of involving private companies in partnership with public and voluntary agencies have yet to be seriously explored in Ireland.

One of the most obvious findings by the authors relates to the extant expertise and energy of NGOs working in localised areas to deliver holiday opportunities to marginalised groups. To a large extent, this work operates without any over-arching policy direction or guidance from national arenas. It goes largely unrecognised and certainly goes unrewarded beyond the appreciation shown by those directly affected. The existing infrastructure, expertise and status of NGOs working at holiday provision in local communities is a resource to be harnessed while also preserving the distinctiveness of individual NGOs.

Research elsewhere has shown that a singular or predominant reliance on voluntary efforts has a number of disadvantages (Hadley & Hatch, 1981; Leat, 1981), including uneven distribution of resources both geographically and socially and service being biased towards groups with popular appeal, such as children and the disabled. Furthermore, standards of services tend to vary and the supply of funds can be irregular and *ad hoc*. All of these findings are highly applicable to the existing Irish situation. Existing provision is highly localised, uneven and many elements in its operation are inconsistent. There are indications that demand outstrips supply and that certain cohorts of the population are being excluded from the holidays provided.

Equally problematic at present is the *ad hoc* and informal way in which much of the public sector intervention is structured. Relationships between agencies vary from place to place. Too often linkages are dependent on individual local knowledge or personal connections. Yet, the potential to improve the service to target groups through improved coordination, linkages and joined-up thinking is all too obvious.

Prioritising an integrated approach to supply

An integrated approach to supply is critical. An important finding is that all of the agencies which are active in promoting participation in annual holidaying are also involved in multiple anti-poverty services and supports. In this, Ireland is unusual in an EU context.

A second important finding in this respect is that among the array of services and supports provided by the agencies (whether non-governmental or public), investment in the provision of holidays is accorded low priority. Key informants spoke of constantly having to make the case for 'ring-fencing' or defending budgets and resources for holiday provision.

It is therefore argued that a need exists for actors and agencies to recognise the role that access to holidays can play as one part of a broader set of strategies devised to combat social exclusion. Equally, there is a need to identify ways of integrating holiday services and supports into overall and ongoing support provision. In terms of policy development, these findings indicate a need to consider ways of integrating and coordinating activities in a strategic manner.

Conclusion

While undertaking research leading to this paper, the authors became increasingly aware of the disparity in Ireland between the tourism and social justice spheres, both of which have a role to play in developing tourism for all. While there has been recognition and commitment to sustainable development at Irish policy level since the mid-1990s, environmental issues have received a disproportionate level of attention, to the neglect of social issues.

This disjoint is rooted deep in the philosophy and rationale which underscores activity in the tourism and social justice sectors, respectively. It is critical that this economic and social disjoint is addressed, particularly in the context of long-term sustainable development as a whole. There is a need for profound (perhaps even philosophical) discussion about bringing together economic and social issues which are not irreconcilable. Social and economic added value are inter-related, are mutually supporting and can be achieved in tandem. Indeed, such an approach is necessary for the achievement of sustainable tourism development.

Overall, this paper identifies a range of areas that need attention in order to develop tourism for all policy in an Irish context, including the need to:

- Raise awareness, and deepen understanding, of the value of tourism for all as a measure with potential economic and social benefits.
- Recognise and consider tourism for all in all relevant policy domains, towards its conceptualisation in a holistic manner within the broader policy context.
- Learn from the range of policies and mechanisms that exist across Europe, harnessing the experience and expertise of those countries which have a long-standing record of engagement in the area.
- Recognise and acknowledge the well-established involvement and contribution of volunteers and NGOs, harnessing this within the Irish policy context in a partnership approach with the public and private sectors.
- Consider holidays as an element of integrated service provision, with recognition of the role which access to a holiday can play as one part of a broader set of strategies, both economic and social. An integrated strategic approach to supply within a broader policy context is required to provide support and develop linkages across policy domains and among the range of actors involved in tourism for all measures.
- Acknowledge and accept the integral role of tourism for all in addressing the challenges of sustainable tourism development, both from a social and economic perspective, and broader societal challenges, within an Irish and European context.

There is a need for more research to investigate the phenomenon of tourism for all, particularly in Ireland. The exploratory research conducted by the authors of this paper represents a first attempt to investigate tourism for all in an Irish context, identifying numerous possible avenues for further research. Not least of these is a fuller investigation of the scale and extent of tourism for all provision, in cities and rural areas across the country. Baseline data on, *inter alia*, the number of agencies involved, the degree and nature of linkages between organisations, the range of initiatives and interventions available, the number and type of people being assisted to go on holidays, the overall number of holiday nights provided, and so forth are needed in order to further inform policy development in the area.

Furthermore, the need for cost–benefit analysis, considering both the quantitative economic impact in addition to the qualitative social impact, at both a micro- and macro-level, is important and would certainly be a logical step in supporting the development of tourism for all in Ireland. One of the issues in this regard is that by their very nature, the social issues are difficult if not impossible to quantify and as such, their recognition can be difficult to achieve. Similarly, as the impact and benefits of holidays are many and diverse, indirect economic benefits are difficult to quantify. Available empirical evidence, including research undertaken in the Irish context, has focused largely on qualitative benefits. Quantifiable economic evidence is available in countries such as Spain and France and the Flanders region in Belgium outlining the positive economic impacts accruing from tourism for all. Evidence of such economic benefit in an Irish context would strengthen the tourism for all agenda in Ireland, in tandem with the recognition of the social value of such initiatives. This is particularly important in the current challenging economic climate.

There has been limited recognition and acknowledgement of the social value of holidaying in Ireland, particularly to those sectors of society experiencing poverty and social exclusion. Few actors in Ireland, beyond a number of NGOs active in the anti-poverty domain, recognise this to be a problem. This paper argues that a need exists for policy-makers and practitioners active within social welfare, economic, health, education and tourism domains to acknowledge that holiday participation can yield a series of benefits at personal, inter-personal and societal levels. By extension, there is a need for a fuller awareness of how social exclusion from holiday-taking creates a series of negative social, cultural and economic outcomes. Addressing this situation is important if, following Erikson (2007, p. 265), policy-makers are interested to ensure that Ireland becomes 'not only a richer but also a better society to live in' while Ireland becomes a country 'where people not only earn more but also have better lives'.

Furthermore, lack of attention to the social and economic value of tourism for all represents a barrier to achieving sustainable tourism development in an Irish context. Unless Irish tourism policy-makers turn their attention to 'making holidays available to all', then Irish tourism will fail to meet at least one of the eight key tourism sustainability challenges identified by the European Commission (2007) and further fail to realise the existing Irish policy commitment to sustainable tourism development.

Acknowledgements

The authors would like to acknowledge the Combat Poverty Agency, Policy Research Initiative in Ireland, which funded the research which has led to the preparation of this paper.

References

Brimacombe, M. (2003). Wish you were here? *New Start Magazine*. Retrieved August 24, 2009, from www.newstartmaga.co.uk/holidays.html.
Central Statistics Office. (2007). *EU Survey on Income and Living Conditions 2006*. Cork, UK: Author.
Central Statistics Office. (2009). *EU Survey on Income and Living Conditions 2008*. Cork, Ireland: Author.
Cohen, S., & Taylor, L. (1992). *Escape attempts: The theory and practice of resistance to everyday life*. London: Routledge.
Corlyon, J., & La Placa, V. (2006). *Holidays for families in need*. London: Policy Research Bureau.
Dawson, D. (1988). Leisure studies and the definition of poverty. *Leisure Studies*, 7(3), 221–231.
Department of the Environment. (1997). *Sustainable development: A strategy for Ireland*. Dublin, Ireland: Stationary Office.
English Tourist Board. (1976). *Holidays: The social need*. London: Author.
English Tourist Board. (1985). *Holiday motivations – Special report*. London: Author.
English Tourist Board. (1989). *Tourism for all*. London: Author.
Erikson, R. (2007). Soaring in the best of times? In T. Fahey, H. Russell, & C.T. Whelan (Eds.), *Best of times: The social impact of the Celtic tiger* (pp. 265–276). Dublin, Ireland: Institute of Public Administration.
Eurobarometer. (1998). *Europeans and their holidays*. Brussels, Belgium: European Commission DG XXIII.
European Commission. (2001). *Outcome of the European Ministerial Conference 'Tourism for All'*, Retrieved May 25, 2006, from http://europa.eu.int/comm./enterprise/services/tourism/policyareas/bruges_conference.htm.
European Commission. (2007). *Action for more sustainable European tourism*. Brussels, Belgium: European Commission DG XXIII.
European Commission. (2009). *CALYPSO tourism preparatory action*. Brussels, Belgium: European Commission DG XXIII.
European Economic and Social Committee. (2003, October 29). *Socially sustainable tourism for everyone. Opinion INT/173*. Brussels, Belgium: Author.
European Economic and Social Committee. (2006). *Social Tourism in Europe – Opinion of the EESC*. Brussels, Belgium: EESC.

Ghate, D., & Hazel, N. (2002). *Parenting in poor environments: Stress, support and coping*. London, UK: Jessica Kingsley.

Gilbert, D., & Abdullah, J. (2002). A study of the impact of the expectations of a holiday on an individual's sense of well-being. *Journal of Vacation Marketing*, *8*(4), 352–361.

Godfrey, K. (1996). The evolution of tourism planning in Cyprus. *The Cyprus Review*, *8*(1), 111–133.

Government of Ireland. (2007). National Development Plan 2007–2013. *Transforming Ireland: A better quality of life for all*. Dublin, Ireland: Stationery Office.

Hadley, R., & Hatch, R. (1981). *Social welfare and the failure of the state*. Boston, MA: Allen and Unwin.

Hall, C.M. (2005). *Tourism: Rethinking the social science of mobility*. Harlow: Prentice Hall.

Haukeland, J. (1990). Non-travellers: The flip side of motivations. *Annals of Tourism Research*, *17*(2), 172–184.

Haulot, A. (1981). Social tourism: Current dimensions and future developments. *International Journal of Tourism Management*, *2*(3), 207–212.

Hazel, N. (2005). Holidays for children and families in need. *Children and Society*, *19*(3), 225–236.

Hobson, J.S.P., & Dietrich, U.C. (1994). Tourism, health and quality of life: Challenging the responsibility of using the traditional tenets of sun, sea, sand and sex in tourism marketing. *Journal of Travel and Tourism Marketing*, *3*(4), 21–38.

Hughes, H. (1991). Holidays and the economically disadvantaged. *Tourism Management*, *12*(3), 193–196.

Jolin, L. (2004). *L'ambition du Tourisme Social: Un tourisme pour tous, durable et solidaire*. Retrieved May 26, 2006, from www.bits-int.org.

Lanquar, R. (1996). Is there an urgent need to redefine social tourism? *Espaces (Paris)*, *137*, 40–43.

Leat, D. (1981). *Voluntary or statutory collaboration: Rhetoric of reality?* London: Bedford Square Press.

Lewis, E. (2001). *Evaluation of the benefits of recreational holidays for young people in public care*. London: National Children's Bureau.

Maître, B., Nolan, B., & Whelan, C. (2006). *Reconfiguring the measurement of deprivation and consistent poverty in Ireland*, ESRI Policy Research Series No. 58, February.

Mannell, R.C., & Iso-Ahola, S.E. (1987). Psychological nature of leisure and tourism experience. *Annals of Tourism Research*, *14*(2), 314–331.

Micklewright, J., & Stewart, K. (2001). Poverty and social exclusion in Europe. *New Economy*, *8*(2), 104–109.

Minnaert, L., Maitland, R., & Miller, G. (2009). Tourism and social policy – The value of social tourism'. *Annals of Tourism Research*, *36*(2), 316–334.

Minnaert, L., Stacey, J., Quinn, B., & Griffin, K. (2010). Social tourism for low income groups: Benefits in a UK and Irish context. In N. Morgan & S. Cole (Eds.), *Tourism and inequality* (pp. 126–142). CABI: Wallingford.

Office for Social Inclusion. (2007). *National action plan for social inclusion 2007–2016*. Dublin, Ireland: Author.

Organisation for Economic Cooperation and Development. (2004). *National tourism policy review of Ireland*. Paris, France: Author.

Quinn, B., & Stacey, J. (2010). The benefits of holidaying for children experiencing social exclusion: Recent Irish evidence. *Leisure Studies*, *29*(1), 29–52.

Richards, G. (1998). Time for a holiday? Social rights and international tourism consumption. *Time and Society*, *7*(1), 145–160.

Seaton, A.V. (1992). Social stratification in tourism choice and experience since the War: Part 1. *Tourism Management*, *13*(1), 106–111.

Sharpley, R. (2003). Rural tourism and sustainability – a critique. In D. Hall, L. Roberts, & M. Mitchell (Eds.), *New directions in rural tourism*. Aldershot: Ashgate Publishing Limited.

Shaw, G., & Williams, A. (2002). *Critical issues in tourism: A geographical perspective*. Oxford: Blackwell Publishing.

Smith, V. (1998). *The relationship between poverty, holiday taking and social policy*. Manchester: Manchester Metropolitan University.

Smith, V., & Hughes, H. (1999). Disadvantaged families and the meaning of the holiday. *International Journal of Tourism Research*, *1*(2), 23–133.

Temowetsky, G.W. (1983). Holiday taking and socio-economic status in Australia. *Leisure Studies*, *2*(1), 31–44.

Tourism Policy Review Group. (2003). *New horizons for Irish tourism*. Dublin, Ireland: Stationary Office.

United Nations. (1948). *Universal declaration of human rights*. Paris, France: United Nations General Assembly.

United Nations World Tourism Organisation. (1999). *Global code of ethics for tourism*. Madrid, Spain: World Tourism Organisation.

United Nations World Tourism Organisation. (2004). Sustainable Development of Tourism Conceptual Definition. Retrieved September 25, 2008, from www.world-tourism.org/sustainable/concepts.htm.

Van Raaji, W.F., & Francken, D.A. (1984). Vacation decisions, activities and satisfaction. *Annals of Tourism Research*, *11*(1), 101–112.

Voysey, K. (2000). *Just what the doctor ordered*. London: English Tourism Council.

Whelan, C., Layte, R., & Maître, B. (2003). Persistent income poverty and deprivation in the European Union. *Journal of Social Policy*, *32*(1), 1–18.

Wigfall, V. (2004). *Turning lives around*. London: Family Holiday Association.

The role of charities in social tourism

Philippa Hunter-Jones

University of Liverpool Management School, Liverpool L69 7ZH, UK

The aim of this paper is to examine the extent to which charities contribute to social tourism activity and the forms which these contributions might take. The needs of those disadvantaged because of personal, economic or social circumstances are central to the enquiry. An earlier piece by Turner, Miller and Gilbert (2001), which explores the broader role of UK charities in the tourism industry, suggesting them to operate *outside*, *within* and *above* the tourism industry, provides a framework for initial consideration. Primary qualitative data collected from 20 charitable organisations are considered next with fundraising, accommodation support and signposting activities, all common areas of charitable involvement, noted. This paper concludes by extending the earlier framework presented by Turner et al. (2001) [The role of UK charities and the tourism industry. *Tourism Management*, *22*, 463–472] to include a *surrogate* dimension. It also comments upon the piecemeal support offered by charities to disadvantaged consumers, makes the case for the charitable and private sector tourism industry to seek ways of working together in the future and offers some tentative suggestions for future research. These suggestions are linked to both the research methodology employed in the study and the need for further research linked to consumer attitudes towards charitable giving.

Introduction

Earlier work by Smith and Hughes (1999, p. 123), exploring the meaning of the holiday to disadvantaged families, that is, those 'rarely able to go on holiday because of personal, economic and social circumstances', found the activity to be of particular significance to the families investigated, as it generated feelings of normality and escapism while making a positive contribution to relationships and health too. These authors claim that charities have a significant role to play in facilitating tourism activity for the disadvantaged, going as far as to suggest that 'in the UK, [holiday] assistance to the disadvantaged is largely confined to grants from charitable bodies such as the FHA [Family Holiday Association]' (Smith & Hughes, 1999, p. 132), a charitable organisation we return to within the literature review.

Literature searches of the tourism–charity relationship unearth a paucity of associated researches. One particularly focused paper is presented by Turner, Miller and Gilbert (2001), who provide a framework for charity involvement in tourism classifying this involvement into those which operate *outside, within* and *above* the tourism industry. Identifying travel as a tool for charitable fundraising activity, as a means of protecting threatened habitats and as presenting opportunities for volunteering and campaigning, these authors conclude that 'the framework may need to be extended, as such, this research represents a starting point only (...) the whole area of charity involvement in tourism (...) [is] under researched' (Turner et al., 2001, p. 471). This paper aims to build upon (and to an extent challenge and re-interpret) Turner et al.'s (2001) earlier work, this time by exploring particularly the role that charities play in facilitating tourism for all, an angle not explicitly covered in their earlier piece. Adopting the premise that tourism participation represents a necessary part of everyday life, akin to a basic human right (see Higgins-Desbiolles (2006) for a fuller discussion), this paper examines the extent to which charities contribute to social tourism activity for those disadvantaged because of personal, economic or social circumstances and the forms which these contributions take.

This paper uses evidence from both secondary research and interviews with 20 charitable organisations to make its case with the material delivered in three parts. The first part is a literature review that introduces us to the meaning and role of the charitable sector in a general context, considers the challenges facing this sector and provides examples of charitable involvement in tourism activity. The second part is focused upon detailing the methods of data collection adopted, while the third part presents the findings of the research. This paper concludes by extending the earlier framework presented by Turner et al. (2001) to include a *surrogate* dimension. It also comments upon the piecemeal support offered by charities to disadvantaged consumers, makes the case for the charitable and private sector tourism industry to seek ways of working together in the future and offers some tentative suggestions for future research.

Understanding the charitable sector

The aim of this section is to explain what a charity is and to introduce us to some of the overarching issues facing this sector. Founded upon philanthropic principles:

> to qualify as a charity an organization must be for the relief of poverty, or for the advancement of education, or for the advancement of religion, or for other purposes beneficial to the community, not falling under any of the preceding heads. (Charities Digest, 2005, p. viii)

More specifically, a charity can exist for the advancement of health, citizenship and human rights and for the 'relief of those in need by reason of youth, age, ill-health, disability, financial hardship or other disadvantage' (UK Charities Act, 2006). They may operate at a local, national or international level pursing a range of objectives. A notable proportion of charities are linked to international aid, children, cancer, health advocacy and disability, animal protection and the heritage environment (Mintel, 2008).

Seeking an income source remains a challenge and dominates the work of most. While some charities benefit from the pockets of public sector funding, the main charities are funded essentially through donations, legacies, a 'vital, albeit somewhat unpredictable source of income' (Catchpole, 2009, p. 12), and sponsorships, both individual and, increasingly today, corporate sponsorships supported often through the corporate social responsibility programme of an organisation. This programme represents an attempt by the business sector to 'develop a marked non-economic function in society rather than only producing goods and making profits' (Nicolau, 2008, p. 990). The latter means of support is problematic, however. While recent research indicates that charities have enjoyed a rise in major donations through both individual and corporate employee fundraising and direct debit schemes (Mintel, 2008), so too research highlights their vulnerability to changing economic circumstances (Washington & Atkinson, 2009), as corporate sponsors, in particular, struggle to maintain allegiances (Wall Street Journal Europe, 2009).

Threats to the status quo exist beyond short-term market fluctuations though and can be linked to consumer technological engagement, changing patterns of legacies and competition for public good cause giving. Technology has empowered many of us to become small-time traders, posting merchandise onto online auction sites with really very little skill required or regulation demanded and making financial gains from something we may once have given to charity. Legacies are particularly sensitive to property and share prices (Washington & Atkinson, 2009), with consumers modifying their good cause giving accordingly. One demonstration of this change is the increasing number of ageing parents, those most likely to bequeath money to charities through a sense of duty, offering their savings to their children while alive to facilitate their entry onto the property ladder (Mintel, 2008). Competition between charitable causes for public support continues to grow. For instance, in the UK, the relationship between charities and the National Lottery has been volatile since the latter was introduced in November 1994. Commenting upon the first 5 years of the competition, Smith and Higgins (2000) noted that 5% of adults admitted to altering their patterns of charitable donations in favour of the Lottery. While these threats do not necessarily mean that any particular *cause* is suffering, what they do signal is that the traditional charity structure and funding are either changing or need to change to survive. Perhaps, one of the most notable changes that we may witness in the future is the move away from a sector mainly supported by public funding to one in which the private sector is likely to play a greater role.

Charities have responded to changing circumstances in a number of innovative ways (Broadbridge & Parsons, 2003a, 2003b). There has been a flurry of activity linked to a growing *professionalisation* 'a catchall phrase embracing a plethora of unexamined changes (...) encompasses image enforcement, shop standardisation, segmentation and specialisation' (Broadbridge & Parsons, 2003a, p. 719), invariably head office driven and seen to be spreading through the retail arm of the charitable sector (Broadbridge & Parsons, 2003a, 2003b; Horne, 2000; Parsons, 2002). Some have adopted a route linked to celebrity endorsement (Byrne, Whitehead, & Breen, 2003; Erdogan, 1999; Lear, Runyan, & Whitaker, 2009), although early evidence suggests that consumers are suspicious of the reason for celebrity involvement (Mintel, 2008). Another more fruitful route is through embracing Web 2.0 technologies. Projects in this respect have seen a number of them launching online charity shops (The Times, 2008), facilitating online donation memorials, pay-per-click campaigns, e-card schemes, payroll-linked donations, sifting through donations received to search for good quality merchandise to sell online through auction sites (e.g. www.ebay.co.uk and www.auctionmystuff.org) and others starting to take advantage of social networking sites (Marketing, 2008). Somewhat ironically, such progress has resulted in a new 'challenge' for the sector, how 'not to appear too commercialised and therefore outside the realm of what the public believes a charity should be, whilst simultaneously rais[ing] as much money as possible' (Turner et al., 2001, p. 464).

The tourism–charitable sector relationship

The aim of this section is to review the different ways in which the tourism literature has profiled the tourism–charity relationship to date. It is delivered in two parts. First, it reviews the work presented by Turner et al. (2001), which provides an overarching framework of charity involvement in tourism claiming them to exist *outside*, *within* and *above* the tourism industry. This work mirrors the majority of related literatures, examples of which are referred to within the discussion. Second, it attempts to piece together evidence of charitable involvement in social tourism more specifically.

Framework of tourism–charity involvement

For Turner et al. (2001, p. 464), those 'on the *outside* of the tourism industry, who use tourism solely as a means of fund-raising, are often the charities with the most access to fund-raising and investment management advice'. The link with adventure holidays is noted and examples cited include OXFAM (www.oxfam.org.uk), Guide Dogs for the Blind Association (GDBA) (www.guidedogs.org.uk) and the National Society for the Prevention of Cruelty to Children (NSPCC) (www.nspcc.org.uk). That this form of activity is increasing is an implicit assumption in the growing body of literatures, which profiles the backpacker community worldwide (see, for instance, Reichel, Fuchs, & Uriely, 2009).

'Charities that operate *within* the tourism industry do so to fulfil goals of education, scientific research and conservation; in many cases to find alternative sources of economic development for areas threatened by consumptive resource use' (Turner et al., 2001, p. 466). Examples here include The National Trust (www.nationaltrust.org.uk), Sustrans (www.sustrans.org.uk) and Raleigh International (www.raleighinternational.org). The uniting theme of this group is linked to volunteerism, people volunteer to work for these charities, work which might include conservation and working holidays within the UK and abroad. Sin (2009) and Cousins (2007) examine this angle in their exploration of the relationship between volunteer tourism and charitable donations. Both focus upon the contribution of volunteers to the social capital of a nation, particularly, in developing countries and both use a tourism lens to undertake this analysis. For Cousins (2007), the fact that the 'volunteer tourist' is prepared to pay to become involved in organised conservation work places a responsibility upon the tourism industry facilitating such activities to 'keep the quality of their conservation products high and the volunteer's engagement with nature deep and meaningful' (Cousins, 2007, p. 1020).

The final group of charities which operate *above* the tourism industry are those which 'aim to influence the individual values in society, and ultimately impact public policy decisions (. . .) their actions challenge the agendas that dominate popular thinking in the areas of government tourism policy, industry practices and education for and about tourism' (Turner et al., 2001, p. 468). These charities seek to improve the circumstances of communities and include examples as diverse as lobbyists Tourism Concern (www.tourismconcern.org.uk), End Child Prostitution in Asian Tourism (ECPAT) (www.ecpat.net) and the Whale and Dolphin Conservation Society (www.wdcs.org.uk). While they use tourism to raise money on occasion, much more important to this group are the opportunities tourism presents to raise the profile of the cause in question.

Charitable involvement in social tourism

Collectively, literature suggests that there are two inter-related ways by which charities make a contribution to the social tourism agenda: as a tourism facilitator and as a research facilitator.

As a tourism facilitator

Clough (1999) reviews a week's holiday in Margate, UK, for disadvantaged families organised and funded by the Family Holiday Association (FHA), a charity established (in the

UK) in 1975 'to assist severely deprived families to have a holiday' (Smith & Hughes, 1999, p. 126), which now supports in the region of approximately 1100 UK families a year (Minnaert, Maitland, & Miller, 2009). Similar to the work of Smith and Hughes (1999), Clough (1999) utilises quotes from participants as 'evidence' to demonstrate how holidays can help to rebuild lives and relieve some of the more isolating problems generated through poverty and deprivation. The role of the FHA as a tourism provider is considered, but broader issues linked to the tourism–charity relationship are not addressed at this point.

As a research facilitator

The findings of Clough's work are corroborated by a more recent piece by Minnaert et al. (2009). These authors investigated the holiday-taking experiences of low-income groups, concluding that 'social tourism was found to increase family capital in the short term and social capital (. . .) in the medium term'. Once again, the FHA played a pivotal role in the research, acting as welfare agents, that is, 'support workers, such as health workers, charity workers or social workers, who apply for the holiday on behalf of the participants' (Minnaert et al., 2009, p. 317). The FHA provided the researchers with 40 potential respondents to interview. These respondents all fell within the low-income category but were also considered to be affected by various social problems too 'for example they [might] include carers for disabled children, women who have fled a violent relationship, persons affected by HIV and people with mental health problems' (Minnaert et al., 2009, p. 322). It is difficult to imagine how contact with respondents experiencing such complex circumstances might have been achieved without the FHA link.

This facilitating role, perhaps more aptly described as a gatekeeper role, while not without consequences (see Lee's (1993) comments on conditional research access for further insights here), is indeed an important feature of the work of charities in social tourism research. Further examples of this are provided by the work of Smith and Hughes (1999) and Hunter-Jones (2004). Both articles discuss the holiday-taking experiences of disadvantaged consumers, those economically disadvantaged in the former paper and those experiencing ill-health in the latter paper. Both draw upon charitable organisations to facilitate primary data collection, the FHA and the Joseph Rowntree Charitable Trust (www.jrct.org.uk) responsible for administering the Family Fund (FF) in the former paper and the Malcolm Sargent fund (now Caring for Children with Cancer (CLIC) Sargent, www.clicsargent.org.uk) in the latter paper. Both also highlight a signposting problem in researching charity involvement in tourism in that neither of the papers, or indeed any of the papers reviewed in this article thus far, with the exception of Turner et al. (2001), included the word charity in their title or keywords. Instead, it is more common for reference to a charitable organisation to appear within the text of an article, often as a contributor to a study methodology. Given that the title and keywords are the standard mechanisms upon which database searches operate, it may be reasonably assumed that only a partial picture of the charity–social tourism relationship has been presented in this review so far.

Methodology

The specific intention of this research is to add to our understanding of the tourism–charitable sector relationship by exploring particularly the role that charities play in facilitating tourism for the disadvantaged. Modelling the earlier work of Turner et al. (2001), academic literature searches, web pages, newspapers, magazines, brochures and advertisements all contributed to the secondary research for this study. The keywords searched included charities, tourism, health, leisure, activity breaks, activity camps, activity holidays, non-profit, not-for-profit, voluntary sector, disability, third sector, co-operatives, associations, mutual associations, social enterprise and corporate social responsibility, terms used in varying combinations. One publication that came to light during this review was the regularly updated Charities Digest (2005). This publication categorises 140 charities in the UK (operating at the local, national and international levels) as involved in some manner with the tourism sector. A content analysis of the materials (brochures and websites) produced by these organisations was undertaken, and direct contact was established with 20 charitable organisations whose aim was most closely linked to the notion of encouraging tourism for all. As the results will show, not all charities recognised this role.

All the 20 organisations contacted (Table 1) agreed to take part in the study with semi-structured interviews subsequently conducted to explore the scope and operation of their work, particularly within the context of supporting tourism activity. Due to their geographical spread, the majority of interviews were conducted over the telephone. This was problematic at times as even the use of speaker phone made it difficult to fully record the dialogue. A greater reliance upon note-taking is an inevitable consequence of this approach and should be noted as a potential limitation of the study methodology. Interview data were analysed manually for additional flexibility and insight using template analysis, a technique sometimes referred to as 'codebook analysis' or 'thematic coding' (King, 1998). The technique works on the basis of creating a list of codes or themes (a template) from the textual data (Crabtree & Miller, 1999). Themes emerging through this process were linked to the meaning of the holiday, fundraising, accommodation provision and signposting activities.

Findings

Organisational profile of charitable respondents

Table 1 lists the organisations interviewed within this research. While they primarily reflect local and national charities operating within the UK, some for example, Over the Wall and Children's Wish Foundation, are part of international operations. The scope of their work varied widely, as did the consumer group that they targeted. They included condition-specific charities, for example, Multiple Sclerosis Society, others that operated on age criteria, for example, Age Concern, charities that operated on condition and age criteria, for example, Teenage Cancer Trust and others linked to previous employment activities, for example, Winged Fellowship Trust (now Vitalise). This pattern mirrors the work of the charitable sector more generally too.

Tourism–charity relationship

From the research outset, unpacking the individual tourism–charity relationship proved to be a complex activity. Interviews opened by explaining the aim of the research to respondents and by asking them to suggest a term within this context that they felt most comfortable with using. Only charities directly linked to holidays, for example, FHA, Tourism for All and Holiday Care Service appeared comfortable in being associated with the term 'holiday'. The remaining interviewees chose instead to describe their activities as more in line with offering respite care and short breaks for reasons articulated by the spokesperson for the Winged Fellowship Trust:

Table 1.   Profile of charitable respondents.

Name of the organisation (area of coverage)	Aim of the organisation
Age Concern (UK – National coverage)[a]	The UK's largest charity working with and for older people (www.ageconcern.org.uk)
Arthritis Care (UK – National coverage)	The UK's largest organization working with and for all people who have arthritis (www.arthritiscare.org.uk)
Children's Adventure Farm Trust (CAFT) (UK – Regional coverage)	Providing holidays and activities for terminally ill, chronically sick, disabled and disadvantaged children from all over the north-west (UK) (www. childrensadventurefarm.org)
Children's Wish Foundation (International coverage)	Dedicated to fulfilling a favorite wish for children afflicted with a high risk, life-threatening illness (www. childrenswish.org)
Claire Sadler Trust (UK – Originally regional coverage, now extending)	A charity raising funds to send teenagers on holidays and outings (www.clairesadlerfund.org.uk)
Disaway Trust (UK – National coverage)	Organizes group holidays with physically disabled people (www.disaway.co.uk)
Family Holiday Association (UK – National coverage)	Works to help disadvantaged families get that much needed break away from home (fhaonline.org.uk)
Holiday Care Service[b]	See Tourism for All
Livability (formerly John Grooms Holidays), (UK – National coverage)	Livability is about creating choices for disabled people rather than making choices for them (www.livability.org. uk)
Macmillan Cancer (UK – National coverage)	Provide practical, medical and financial support and push for better cancer care (www.macmillan.org.uk)
Multiple Sclerosis Society (UK – National coverage)	The UK's largest charity for people affected by multiple sclerosis – about 100,000 people in the UK (www. mssociety.org.uk)
Over the Wall (UK – National coverage – with international links)	A charity providing residential activity camps for children and young people affected by serious and life limiting illnesses (www.otw.org.uk)
Starlight Children's Foundation (UK – National coverage)	Brightens the lives of seriously and terminally ill children by granting their wishes and providing hospital entertainment (www.starlight.org.uk)
Teenage Cancer Trust (UK – National coverage)	Devoted to improving the lives of teenagers and young adults with cancer (www.teenagecancertrust.org)
The Disability Foundation (UK – National coverage)	A charity promoting the lives of all disabled people, their families and carers, by supporting them in their desire to live an independent and dignified lifestyle (www.tdf.org. uk)
The Royal National Institute for the Blind (UK – National coverage)	UK's leading charity offering information, support and advice to over two million people with sight loss (www. rnib.org.uk)
Tourism for All (UK – National coverage)[b]	A national charity dedicated to making tourism welcoming to all (www.tourismforall.org.uk)
Tripscope (UK – National coverage)	Helpline for elderly and disabled people (www.tripscope. org.uk)
Vitalise (UK – National coverage)[c]	A national charity providing short breaks (respite care) and other services for disabled people, visually impaired people and carers (www.vitalise.org uk)
Winged Fellowship Trust[c]	See Vitalise

[a]Since merged with Help the Aged to form Age UK.
[b]Since merged to form Tourism for All.
[c]Since merged into Vitalise.

> We are involved in supporting breaks, mainly through grant schemes, for people to rest and relax. We wouldn't think of it as a holiday (...) that sort of thing [referring to the term holiday] undermines the importance of the breaks we support. No we are really about offering respite breaks.

One analysis of this comment suggests that respondents did not see the benefits to health and wellbeing that holidays themselves offer, recognising them instead as merely a frivolous activity. This is interesting given that the Collins Dictionary (Collins, 1999, p. 702) defines respite as 'an interval of rest; a temporary delay', which is closely akin to Graburn's (1983, p. 11) earlier description of tourism as 'one of those necessary structured breaks from ordinary life (...) identified with "re-creation" – the renewal of life, the re-charging of run down elements'. An interesting angle to this debate is offered by the spokesperson for the Disability Foundation who commented at the end of the interview 'I've been involved in organising breaks for a number of years now and yet I never thought of them as holidays before. They are really aren't they?' Whether charities associated themselves with holiday provision or not, as the following discussion will show, their actions and activities did place them in what the tourism industry would commonly recognise as such. Broadly speaking, two types of relationships emerged: Type 1 – charities whose primary purpose is dedicated to holiday-taking support, for example, FHA and Type 2 – charities whose support of holiday-taking is a secondary or even incidental activity, for example, Macmillan Cancer Trust. While some blurring of the boundaries does exist, all were united in their support for disadvantaged consumers.

Fundraising

Fundraising activities played a crucial role for each charity. Money was needed for a variety of purposes such as to sustain everyday living costs, to employ more nurses, to conduct further research and to rebuild hospital facilities. Charities did, in a number of cases, acknowledge that a key part of their fundraising activities was to facilitate a break, albeit often a respite break, for those in need, with the perceived benefits of holidays being a uniting feature of the reason behind this. The Claire Sadler Trust provides one example of this. Set up with the remit of raising funds to send teenagers experiencing serious illness on holidays and outings, a spokesperson commented:

> We take trips really seriously and have managed to fund travel throughout the UK and Europe for many young people (...) it's a really important part of their development (...) it helps to give them self-confidence, raise their self-esteem and give them hope too.

These comments corroborate the earlier findings of Hunter-Jones (2004), who argued that for young people living with cancer, a holiday represented a time of normality and an opportunity for them to rebuild shattered confidences. They were also central to the rationale for supporting 'holidays' offered by the FHA, the Children's Wish Foundation and the Starlight Foundation with terms such as contributing to 'self-confidence', 'fun', 'enjoyment' and 'normality' being common occurrences in conversations.

How charities attempted to raise monies differed from one organisation to another with donations, legacies and corporate sponsorship being common avenues of revenue. What was noticeable though was the number of charities seeking to raise money through sponsored activities. For instance, the spokesperson for the Children's Adventure Farm Trust (CAFT) spoke of raising monies through sponsored bike rides, treks and other such activities to assist them to fully fund breaks at the Adventure Farm base. This approach has some similarities with charities that Turner et al. (2001) claim operate *outside* of the tourism industry, those using tourism as a vehicle for fundraising. A subtle difference exists though. In the case of CAFT, monies raised through this route were then re-invested into facilitating breaks for people and, in effect, directly supporting social tourism actions. In the case of Turner's examples, monies raised through adventure holidays, bike rides and other such means were not necessarily re-invested back into supporting tourism participation, but used instead to fund a whole diversity of activities ranging from guide dogs for the blind to international aid programmes.

For charities linked to social tourism, the ways in which monies were used to support breaks varied. After overheads, the FHA used a significant proportion of monies raised to fund breaks for families. In contrast, the Teenage Cancer Trust and the Multiple Sclerosis Society had a much broader remit of activity to fund including research and medical support. Monies made available for breaks (through grant application schemes) were targeted not only at those in direct medical need but at siblings and parents too for the reasons summarised by a spokesperson for the Teenage Cancer Trust:

> We concentrate mainly upon the patient but you can't neglect their family and friends (…) siblings often have a far worse deal than people realize (…) we have introduced breaks for siblings and friends so that everyone gets some support.

A further approach is illustrated by the Age Concern spokesperson:

> We don't directly fund holidays but the money we do make available can help to offset the cost of a holiday (…) if we can help people to pay their heating and lighting bills then they will have more money left over to spend on leisure activities.

These are clearly all critical contributions. As holidays remain a luxury activity for many, accessing support even indirectly may help to alter the balance and enable participation for a wider population. The paucity of funding for people in need was raised by a number of interview respondents. Interestingly, one area of concern related to the additional costs that people with complex needs face in accessing holiday experiences. A spokesperson for Livability (formerly John Grooms Holidays) commented that 'breaks with special requirements are more expensive and there is a definite lack of choice', a comment further echoed by the Arthritis Care respondent 'we find people struggle to take any breaks as they end up needing to spend more money to pay for specialist accommodation'. Furthermore, just as the majority of charitable funding is tied up with a handful of charities (Mintel, 2008), so too a disparity in funding options arose for different consumer groups. This study found that children and cancer patients were eligible to apply to a greater range of charities than other age groups or those with other health conditions. This inequity was raised by the Disability Foundation, whose spokesperson commented upon the difficulties in accessing funding for those involved in caring for the disadvantaged:

> We have come across breaks for those with a disability however there seems little money in the pot for the carers. There also seems more funding for certain types of disability, such as those with learning disabilities. (The Disability Foundation)

This example highlights well the complexity of funding a break. It also suggests that the disadvantaged may themselves experience different levels of disadvantage too.

Accommodation provision

Accommodation is an integral part of tourism activity. It proved to be an area commonly referred to by respondents. A number of charities spoke of operating their own accommodation for people in need. Macmillan Cancer Trust, for instance, owns and operates Albany Lodge, a hotel with traditional hotel facilities supplemented by access to a team of qualified nurses and doctors. Targeted primarily at people with cancer in southern England, UK, access to the facility is primarily through referral from welfare agents. John Grooms (now Livability) also operates a number of specially adapted hotel facilities targeted primarily at the disabled community and their carers. Generally, hotel accommodation was not that common a facility though, and indeed some organisations that had traditionally run hotels, the Royal National Institute for the Blind (RNIB), for instance, actually spoke of closing them down as a consequence of the UK Disability Discrimination Act (DDA) (1995):

> We used to own and manage two hotels but with the introduction of the DDA we found business was in decline (...) we didn't do any specific research but felt that it was due to hotels in general having to make themselves more accessible. (RNIB)

More common forms of accommodation offered by charities, not too dissimilar to general accommodation provision, are listed in Table 2. Not all charities operated their own facilities. Instead, a number of them spoke of raising monies to fund accommodation in locations outside of their own control, as comments by the FHA illustrate:

> we don't actually have a stock of accommodation (...) it would be unrealistic to fund such (...) a number of years ago we negotiated guest house accommodation in Margate for families in need (...) they went for a week and we got fantastic feedback on how important the break was.

Financially, this approach may be particularly appealing to charities. It may also generate opportunities for corporate social responsibility programmes to play a role in too.

Table 2.   Forms of accommodation offered by charities.

Accommodation type	Charity example
Hotels	Macmillan Cancer (www.macmillan.org.uk), Livability (formerly John Grooms, Holidays) (www.livability.org.uk)
Residential holiday homes	BREAK (www.break-charity.org), Children with Leukaemia (www.leukaemia.org)
Residential homes	Autism Initiatives (www.autisminitiatives.org), Hamelin Trust (www.hamelintrust.org.uk)
Holiday homes	CLAN Cancer Support (www.clanhouse.org), Children with Cancer and Leukaemia Advice and Support for Parents (CCLASP) (www.cclasp.net)
Self-catering chalets	Livability (formerly John Grooms Holidays) (www.livability.org.uk), Scout Holiday Homes Trust (www.scoutbase.org.uk)
Holiday bungalows	Beacon Centre for the Blind (www.beacon4blind.co.uk)
Holiday dialysis centres	The British Kidney Patient Association (www.britishkidney-pa.co.uk)
Holiday camps	Barretstown (www.barretstown.org)
Caravans	Children's Cancer Support Group CHICS (www.chicsonline.org), Dave Lee's Happy Holidays (www.happyholidays.moonfruit.com)
Guest houses	Corrymeela Community (www.corrymeela.org)
Holiday villas	Christian Lewis Trust (www.christianlewistrust.org)
Boats	Ellen Macarthur Trust (ellenmacarthurtrust.org)

Signposting

During fundraising-linked conversations, a number of issues linked to the signposting activities of charities emerged. A number of them spoke of how, if they were unable to provide funding through their own organisation, they were able to point people in the direction of other sources of monies and, in some cases, also provide support to complete the application forms attached to the process:

> we can always help in some way (…) even without funding as such we can still explain what options there are out there and help those in need to try and access them. (Age Concern)

This facilitation process was indeed a key area of work identified within the majority of interview responses. All interviewees claimed to contribute to the respite experience with many suggesting that they played an integral role in introducing the idea of a break, suggesting possible choices and signposting information sources, particularly linked to funding, accommodation and transport choices.

Significantly, and in contrast to Turner et al.'s (2001) work, mention of consulting or working with the tourism industry or private sector more widely was notably limited to Hoseasons (www.hoseasons.co.uk, a holiday operator covering the UK and Europe) and Butlins (www.butlins.com, holiday parks in the UK). Whether charities operating in this context are reticent to work with mainstream international tour operators or vice versa remains unclear at this point, as no respondent offered a reason for this situation and it is left to the broader comments made by the spokesperson for the Holiday Care Service to throw some light on the situation:

> One of the biggest challenges charities face is trying to find the time to keep on top of information sources. Take holidays, they include so many different parts to them that planning takes some time. There isn't a good relationship between the holiday industry and charities (…) the industry is so sensitive about their pricing strategy that it's not surprising they are reticent to share information with other organizations (…). Charities need help from specialists but at the moment aren't really getting that support.

Beyond this, holiday-taking constraints identified among respondents included the complexity of encouraging people to think about taking a break and supporting them through, what for many people, can be an arduous planning and organising process. To support the process, seven charities had invested in leisure-related training activities, which included training staff to make holiday bookings (e.g. Vitalise), inspection team training, linked to the UK National Accessible Scheme (e.g. Tourism for All – formerly the Holiday Care Service) and observation of holiday destinations for the specialist market (e.g. Disaway Trust), for marketing (e.g. Tourism for All) and for unspecified reasons (e.g. Tripscope). The nature of signposting support offered varied from organisation to organisation with many focusing their often limited break-linked literature sources upon accommodation choices, transport choices, financial support (i.e. funding options and where to apply to) and the signposting of alternative types of breaks available.

Conclusions

This paper sets out to examine the role that charities play in social tourism. From a secondary research position, it quickly became apparent that a paucity of researches exists considering this relationship. The principle academic source utilised to structure this review was the work by Turner et al. (2001), which outlines the role of charities *outside, within* and *above* the tourism sector. This work most commonly makes the link between charities and ethical/responsible dimensions of tourism at a community level but stops short of directly considering whether charities might also facilitate tourism for all.

The key empirical findings confirm that, in spite of operating on quite limited budgets and without necessary access to training, economies of scale, resources or even recognition for the role that they play, charities often play a fundamental role in supporting tourism activity for disadvantaged consumers. Charities contributing to this study were found to inspire travel, present options and surmount problems, particularly in relation to accommodation, funding and signposting activities for those experiencing personal, economic and social disadvantage. In these circumstances, the charity is not working *within*, *outside* or *above* the tourism industry. It is the tourism industry. The addition of a further *surrogate* category, that is, 'a person or thing acting as a substitute' (Collins, 1999, p. 841), to Turner et al.'s (2001) earlier framework would help to capture this dimension of charitable involvement in tourism.

The study findings also present us with a particularly tough challenge to embrace. For disadvantaged consumers to be supported more fully, and indeed equally in the future, the charitable and private sectors need to work more closely together. Charities do not have a responsibility to attend to the needs of all consumers. Instead, charities are selective in who they help, with their choice being dependent upon the cause in question. Consequently, the support offered to disadvantaged consumers by this sector represents quite a piecemeal affair: some age groups and conditions are more likely to gain support than others; monies available may vary widely and areas that money can be spent on may vary widely too. Much of the support currently offered by the charitable sector relies solely upon resources drawn from this sector. The tourism industry, by its focus and sheer volume of operations, is extremely well placed to provide support to the charitable sector – and indeed already does in some contexts, ethical/responsible tourism particularly, as Turner et al.'s (2001) work demonstrated. The challenge that we now face is seeking ways to extend this relationship further and to bridge the gap between these sectors, so that both, and the consumer, will be able to enjoy the mutual benefits that such a relationship might well generate. Smith and Hughes (1999, p. 132) alluded to this when they suggested that 'any further strategies from the state for widening participation, in the current economic climate, are unlikely and it will fall to the industry itself and voluntary charitable bodies to do this'. Ten years on, the means of achieving this are within our grasp. Opportunities presented within the corporate social responsibility literature, for instance, present a useful starting point.

Agenda for future research

This work has a number of limitations, which themselves represent an agenda for future research. It has focused upon the UK perspective and would now benefit from being tested within other geographical contexts too. The paucity of existing data has given rise to what really can best be described as a scoping study, only the surface of the relationship has been investigated. The scope for further work linked to social enterprises and similar business models is considerable. Equally, the consumer perspective is ripe for further consideration. The values, beliefs and reasons for consumers turning to charities for holiday-taking support remain largely neglected at this point. Similarly, no attention has been paid at all as to how the consumer themselves might feel about having to turn to the third sector for such support. Further research could usefully examine whether receiving charitable support impacts upon the tourism experience or itself generates psychological consequences for those at the sharp end of this. Given the comments noted in a recent Charity Commission report, 'according to a study by the Charity Commission, more than a quarter of UK adults would be embarrassed to receive free help from a charity'(Charity Finance, 2009), this perspective may be far more significant than this study has been able to appreciate.

Acknowledgements

The author would like to thank both Joanne Mellor for her help in the initial data collection and all respondents who took the trouble to be involved in the study.

References

Broadbridge, A., & Parsons, E. (2003a). UK charity retailing: Managing in a newly professionalized sector. *Journal of Marketing Management, 19,* 719–748.

Broadbridge, A., & Parsons, E. (2003b). Still serving the community? The professionalization of the charity retail sector. *International Journal of Retail and Distribution Management, 31*(8), 418–427.

Byrne, A., Whitehead, M., & Breen, S. (2003). The naked truth of celebrity endorsement. *British Food Journal, 105*(4–5), 288–296.

Catchpole, D. (2009). Legacy disputes. *New Law Journal Charities Appeal Supplement, Summer,* 12–13.

Charities Digest. (2005). *Charities Digest 2006* (112th ed.). London: Waterloo Professional Publishing.

Charity Finance. (2009, February 4). Charity commission: One in four people 'embarrassed' to be helped by charities. *Charity Finance, Third Sector Magazine*: Retrieved February 11, 2009, from http://www.thirdsector.co.uk/news.

Clough, J. (1999, May 1). Give them the break of their lifetime. *Telegraph Travel*, p. TII.

Collins (1999). *Paperback English Dictionary.* Glasgow, UK: HarperCollins Publishers.

Cousins, J.A. (2007). The role of UK-based conservation tourism operators. *Tourism Management, 28,* 1020–1030.

Crabtree, B.F., & Miller, W.L. (1999). *Doing qualitative research* (pp. 163–177, 2nd ed.). London, UK: Sage Publications.

Disability Discrimination Act (DDA). (1995). *The Disability Discrimination Act 1995 (Amendment) Regulations 2003 – Online document.* Retrieved October 30, 2008, from http://www.opsi.gov.uk/si/si2003/20031673.htm.

Erdogan, Z. (1999). Celebrity endorsement: A literature review. *Journal of Marketing Management, 15*(4), 291–314.

Graburn, N. (1983). The anthropology of tourism. *Annals of Tourism Research, 10,* 9–33.

Higgins-Desbiolles, F. (2006). More than an "industry": The forgotten power of tourism as a social force. *Tourism Management, 27*(6), 1192–1208.

Horne, S. (2000). The charity shop: Purpose and change. *International Journal of Nonprofit and Voluntary Sector Marketing, 5*(2), 113–124.

Hunter-Jones, P. (2004). Young people, holiday-taking and cancer – an exploratory study. *Tourism Management, 25,* 249–258.

King, N. (1998). Template analysis. In G. Symon & C. Cassell (Eds.), *Qualitative methods and analysis in organizational research: A practical guide.* London: Sage Publications Ltd.

Lear, K.E., Runyan, R.C., & Whitaker, W.H. (2009). Sports celebrity endorsements in retail products advertising. *International Journal of Retail and Distribution Management, 37*(4), 308–321.

Lee, R.M. (1993). *Doing research on sensitive topics.* London: Sage Publications Ltd.

Marketing. (2008, September 10). Oxfam posts £21m FY profits. *Marketing Magazine.* Retrieved December 12, 2010 from http://www.marketingmagazine.co.uk/news/articles.

Minnaert, L., Maitland, R., & Miller, G. (2009). Tourism and social policy. The value of social tourism. *Annals of Tourism Research, 36*(2), 316–334.

Mintel. (2008, March). *Charities UK.* London: Mintel Market Intelligence Publications.

Nicolau, J.L. (2008). Corporate social responsibility. Worth-creating activities. *Annals of Tourism Research*, *35*(4), 990–1006.

Parsons, E. (2002). Charity retail: Past, present and future. *International Journal of Retail and Distribution Management*, *30*(12), 586–594.

Reichel, A., Fuchs, G., & Uriely, N. (2009). Israeli Backpackers. *Annals of Tourism Research*, *36*(2), 222–246.

Sin, H.L. (2009). Volunteer tourism – "Involve me and I will learn". *Annals of Tourism Research*, *36*(3), 480–501.

Smith, W., & Higgins, M. (2000). Cause-related marketing: Ethics and the ecstatic. *Business and Society*, *39*(3), 304–322.

Smith, V., & Hughes, H. (1999). Disadvantaged families and the meaning of the holiday. *International Journal of Tourism Research*, *1*(2), 123–133.

The Times. (2008, October 10). Online trading nets Oxfam £5m. *The Times*, p. 4.

Turner, R., Miller, G., & Gilbert, D. (2001). The role of UK charities and the tourism industry. *Tourism Management*, *22*, 463–472.

UK Charities Act. (2006). *Part 1: Meaning of "Charity" and "Charitable Purpose". Charities Act 2006 (c.50) – Online document.* Retrieved October 30, 2008, from http://www.opsi.gov.uk/acts/acts2006/ukpga_20060050_en_2.

Wall Street Journal Europe. (2009, April 7). Recession hits UK charity sector. *Wall Street Journal Europe*. Retrieved December 12, 2010, from http://online.wsj.com/article/SB.

Washington, J., & Atkinson, H. (2009). Is big always beautiful? *New Law Journal Charities Appeal Supplement*, Summer, 6–7.

Social tourism in Hungary: from trade unions to cinema tickets

László Puczkó[a] and Tamara Rátz[b]

[a]Xellum Ltd, 1051 Budapest, Október 6. u. 14, Hungary; [b]Tourism Department, Kodolányi János University of Applied Sciences, 8000 Székesfehérvár, Fürdő u. 1, Székesfehérvár, Hungary

The concept of social tourism is not new for Hungary. In the socialist era, social tourism took place mostly in mountain, lake-side or spa destinations, as a part of the social services supported by (state owned) companies and trade unions. The facilities, i.e. accommodation establishments of often low quality, were run by companies or trade unions. Employees, union members and their families were eligible to visit these premises. These trips were either free or heavily subsidised. Following the changes around 1990, the old support system collapsed. This system was replaced by the so-called supported holiday system. Social tourism establishments were either privatised or closed down. The role and power of trade unions diminished, the ministry's budget was cut and reorganised significantly. Organisations and companies allocated lower amounts for social benefits and gradually removed inherited obligations, i.e. social tourism. The paper discusses the development and transformation of social tourism in Hungary: from its origins to today's uncertain situation. Social tourism has undergone significant changes in the last decade, leading to a wider scale of supported services as well as increased demand for such services. As a consequence, in 2010, the state has introduced new measures to regulate the market, the end results of which are unforeseeable yet.

Introduction

Tourism has the potential to contribute to the wellbeing of tourists by providing them with restorative holiday experiences that fulfil a wide range of human needs (Higgins-Desbiolles, 2006). Holiday participation may improve physical and mental health and help families develop positive relationships. Participation in leisure tourism may contribute to greater social inclusion through giving all members of society, regardless of their financial circumstances, the opportunity to relax, gain new experiences, spend quality time with their family or get to know the world (Minnaert, 2007).

According to the Manila Declaration by the World Tourism Organization (1980), the right to access to holidays is a natural consequence of the right to work, and it is recognised as an aspect of the fulfilment of the human being by the Universal Declaration of Human Rights. These rights can be interpreted to entail the duty of societies to provide practical,

61

effective and non-discriminatory access to leisure, holidays, travel and tourism for its citizens.

From this point of view, social tourism is an objective which society should pursue in the interest of those unprivileged citizens who are unable to exercise their right to rest (Bhatia, 2006). According to the International Bureau of Social Tourism (BITS in EESC, 2006), social tourism is 'all the concepts and phenomena resulting from the participation in tourism of low-income sectors of the population, made possible through well defined social measures'. The definition also attempts to delineate the main stakeholders in social tourism development: '... is organised in some countries by associations, cooperatives and trade unions and is designed to make travel accessible to the highest number of people, particularly the most underprivileged sectors of the population' (European Commission in EESC, 2006).

Social tourism constitutes an activity whenever three conditions are met: members of certain social groups are unable to fully exercise the right to tourism, due to, for example, economic conditions, physical or mental disability, personal or family isolation, reduced mobility or geographical difficulties such as lack of access to public transportation among isolated village- and farm-dwellers. A public or private institution, a company, a trade union or simply an organised group of people decide to take action to overcome or reduce the obstacle which prevents persons from exercising their right to tourism, and this action is effective and actually helps the affected people to participate in tourism in a manner which respects the values of sustainability, accessibility and solidarity (European Commission in EESC, 2006).

According to the Western European model, social tourism development typically aims to offer services at attractive prices to persons who would otherwise be excluded from tourism. A further objective may be to promote authentic tourist locations and to organise sustainable holiday stays which focus on social, learning, cultural and sports components (Ryan, 2002). Social tourism has been the key to the development of certain isolated regions, by reviving the local economy through the facilitation of domestic travel and the stimulation of revenue creation at domestic destinations (Poy, 2003). Social tourism for families also strengthens the relations among family members, particularly between parents and children, thus contributing to the socialisation of children (Minnaert, 2007). In the socialist countries, however, tourism development was very specifically geared to serving political purposes, including the provision of rest and relaxation for the workers in order to enable their future production in the 'construction of socialism', as well as using tourism as a method of socialist education of young people or fostering solidarity by touring fellow socialist countries (Allcock & Przeclawski, 1990). It has to be added though, that despite the differences in political ideology, this underlying idea was also used by some Western European countries, e.g. in Germany during the Third Reich, a holiday scheme was developed to ensure workers' productivity (Spode, 2004).

Tourism in Hungary

In Hungary, tourism is one of the key economic activities: the industry's direct contribution to the country's gross domestic product exceeds 5%, while the direct and indirect contribution together is approximately 9%. Based on the latest available data of the Hungarian Central Statistical Office, in 2005 tourism provided direct employment for 303,000 people (8% of the active population), while the associated industries employed a further 180,000 persons (altogether 13%) (Hungarian Central Statistical Office in Hungarian National Tourist Office (HNTO), 2009).

Table 1 summarises the main data on domestic tourism registered at commercial accommodation which provides the superstructure for social tourism consumption. In 2008, domestic guests accounted for 49.9% of all guest nights spent at commercial accommodation facilities.

The development of social tourism in Hungary

The development of social tourism in Hungary, similarly to other members of the East-Central European socialist block (Jordan, 2006), followed the ideological principles as well as the practical *modus operandi* of the political system. Throughout Europe, many governments have integrated social tourism into their social welfare policies over the past 50 years. Schemes generally included state-supported services to provide and promote affordable holidays and recreation for disadvantaged groups. However, during the early development stages in the socialist system in Hungary, the introduction of social tourism mainly provided access to otherwise privileged groups (party and trade union officials and members, outstanding factory workers, as well as their families). As the capacity of social tourism increased during the 1970s and early 1980s, the range of beneficiaries also expanded, but the highest quality facilities were still mainly available for the advantaged elite. It was only the political–economic transition process following the collapse of the socialist system in 1989/1990 that resulted in the emergence of a new kind of social tourism system that indeed favours the underprivileged social groups.

Social tourism in Hungary developed on the basis of the trade union movement. After the Second World War, trade unions took over formerly privately owned guesthouses, hotels and castles that were taken into state property in order to provide members with their 'well-deserved' rest and leisure (Michalkó, 2007). A so-called Holiday Centre was established in April 1949 in order to distribute the holiday vouchers that workers could exchange for all inclusive, but generally rather mediocre quality, 1- or 2-week holidays

Table 1. Domestic arrivals and guest nights at commercial accommodation in Hungary, 2007–2008.

	2007	2008	2008/2007
Arrivals	4,023,000	4,135,000	+2.8%
Guest nights	9,958,000	9,965,000	+0.1%
Guest nights in hotels	6,120,737	6,254,495	+2.2%
5 star hotels	161,463	185,275	+14.7%
4 star hotels	2,036,724	2,227,800	+9.4%
3 star hotels	3,060,435	3,011,553	−1.6%
2 star hotels	528,559	556,046	+5.2%
1 star hotels	333,556	273,821	−17.9%
Spa hotels	1,341,002	1,338,952	−0.2%
Wellness hotels	1,046,565	1,207,709	+15.4%
Guesthouses	1,540,977	1,539,787	−0.1%
Tourist hostels	609,466	547,050	−10.2%
Youth hostels	538,127	462,424	14.1%
Bungalows	695,070	702,297	+1.0%
Camping sites	453,349	458,830	+1.2%
Average length of stay (nights)	2.5	2.4	−2.6%
Domestic accommodation revenue (HUF million)	49,589	52,904	+6.1%

Source: HCSO in HNTO, 2009.

at a pre-determined holiday centre, oversee the fair and just allocation of funding received from the state, and ensure the adequate provision of holiday services.

In the early years, the conditions prevailing at the social tourism facilities were rather spartan, since a quantitative development approach dominated over qualitative consider-ations. However, the variety and the quality of holiday types available in the framework of social tourism gradually increased during the 1960s, and soon spas and sanatoria were added to the growing list of family and child holiday options. After 1965, even state-supported international trips became an opportunity, mainly for members of the political elite, the destinations being strictly limited to only a few socialist countries (e.g. East Germany or DDR).

This kind of welfare tourism was not exclusively financed by the National Council of Trade Unions (NCTU): co-operatives, state companies and government bodies were also involved.

The number of beneficiaries showed a steady growth over the decades of the social-ist era: while in 1949 only 250,000 state-supported domestic guests were registered, in 1986 at the peak of the social tourism system, their number exceeded 1.4 million, a 560% increase in less than 40 years (Lengyel, Puczkó, & Rátz, 1996) (Figure 1). This reflected both a continuous increase in the state's financial support, and the expan-sion of the state-owned and also state-managed accommodation sector, including hotels, guesthouses and holiday camps administered either by trade unions or by state-owned companies.

The accommodation capacity of social tourism also increased during the period: in the 1980s, the total capacity exceeded 140,000 beds, with 100,000 beds available in hotels and guesthouses, approximately 25% of which was administered by the NCTU (Figure 2). However, following the peak year in 1984, the social accommodation capacity of the trade unions started to decrease, parallel with the trends in state funding (Figure 3). Since in the second half of the 1980s, the NCTU's revenues of state support and guest con-tribution proved to be insufficient to maintain and operate their social tourism system (Lengyel, 1998), an increasing part of their capacity was transferred to commercial

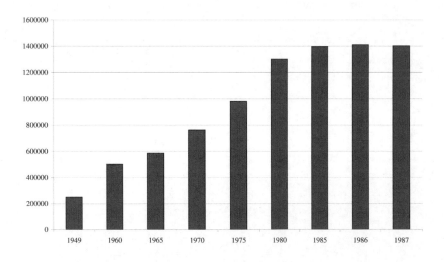

Figure 1.   The number of social tourism beneficiaries between 1949 and 1987 in Hungary.
Source: www.mnua.hu.

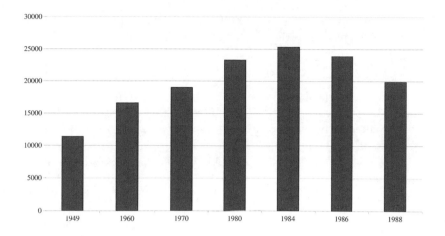

Figure 2.   The accommodation capacity of social tourism administered by trade unions, 1949–1988.
Source: www.mnua.hu.

utilisation, resulting in a permanent decrease in the ratio of welfare guests: in 1996, even at
the recently established Hunguest Hotels, the commerce-oriented successor of the
trade union holiday system, only 36% of the guests received state support (Lengyel
et al., 1996).

As Figure 3 presents, state financial support for social tourism increased steadily until
1982. Afterwards, although the data roughly indicate stagnation in nominal, monetary
value, the real value of this amount decreased significantly, due to the relatively high
inflation rate during the period. The dwindling state support and the increasing operating
costs forced welfare tourism operators to search for additional revenue opportunities.
Therefore, it is hardly surprising that the ratio of 'other revenues' – such as commercial

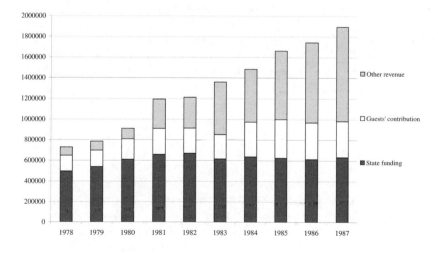

Figure 3.   Revenue of the social tourism system in Hungary between 1978 and 1987.
Source: www.mnua.hu.

accommodation services, meetings and events – in the social tourism system increased from 11 to 48% between 1978 and 1987.

Social tourism after 1989: transformation and development

Following the social, political and economic changes in 1989 (and the years beyond), the base of social tourism collapsed in Hungary (Pohner, 2008). Everything changed drastically. New commercial owners, new market-oriented ideologies appeared, values and objectives shifted from the pretended solidarity of the socialist system to competition. During the first years of the new era, many former social priorities, such as supported travel, became only marginally important. Formerly compulsory membership in trade union membership became voluntary, workers could now freely decide whether they wanted to become or remain trade unions members. As most international and Hungarian private investors also discouraged the organisation of trade unions in their companies, trade unions lost a significant part of their social basis and the social tourism system lost its political–economic foundation. The structure of social tourism, which was mainly based on trade unions and their properties, became unviable (Puczkó & Rátz, 2006).

By 1992, the slowly crumbling social tourism system became almost untenable. The government, together with six trade unions, as part of the repatriation and restructuring process of properties formerly owned by the socialist trade unions, created the Hungarian National Foundation of Recreation (HNFR) (Rátz, 1996). The members of the HNFR were trade unions, the Ministry of Public Welfare and employers, so the Foundation itself was a public rather than a private institution (HNFR, 2008). Although it was becoming clear that the establishment of a brand new system was inevitable, and several stakeholders suggested the introduction of the French holiday cheque system (HCS), adapted to the Hungarian market, the HNFR opted for trying to sustain the already existing structures and mechanisms, but it did not succeed, due to a variety of reasons including the diminishing significance of the trade union movement, the lack of capital and modern management know-how, the increasing quality expectation of customers and the growing competition in the domestic tourism market.

The HNFR was the governing body of social tourism and its main responsibility was to set up a new system which was to be based on the French Holiday Cheque System – this is built on the principles of supporting individual demand as opposed to financing a state-owned service network, free choice for the customer and tax allowances for the participating companies. The details of the new structure and the potential socio-economic impacts of its introduction were assessed by the Tourism Research Centre of the Budapest University of Economic Sciences.[1] Although there was a general consensus in the social tourism industry that the former system was not adequate any more, due to all the above-described social, political and economic changes, and a cheque-based preferential system should be set up in order to remain competitive in the domestic market, the main concern was related to the financing issues. Although the government recognised that the state's direct contribution was essential at the initial stages of the cheque system, the above-mentioned impact assessment study predicted that it would become self-sustaining eventually, or at least generate a positive net impact through increased revenue creation and tax income.

The HNFR, as the owner, established the National Holiday and Property Handling Limited Co. for the administration of the various ex-social tourism properties. In 1993, this limited company was transformed into a public limited company named Hunguest

Corporation as part of the economic restructuring process of the country, i.e. the formerly trade union-run hotels (or more like holiday homes that only partly met the general quality requirements of hotels) formed a new hotel chain in the Hungarian commercial and welfare accommodation market. This chain did not follow the traditional chain hotel model. The 365 properties were of different size, locations and, most importantly, quality. Most of them were either located around Lake Balaton (the largest freshwater lake in Central- and Eastern Europe, and the major holiday region of Hungary), or at thermal and medical spa resorts, while some of them were at mountain resorts. In order to finance its operation, the HNFR relied on a profit from the hotels' operation, since Hunguest Corporation was owned by the HNFR (State Audit Office, 2001).

In 1993, the HNFR divided the 365 properties into two categories: profitable, successful properties to keep and manage, and superfluous properties without a potential for further growth (altogether 104). The latter group was 'given back' to the State Property Agency, the country's privatisation agency that retained responsibility for state property, in order to provide the HNFR with a leaner and competitive portfolio. Altogether, 171 properties were transferred into Hunguest Corporation Trust in 1994. The rest of the properties were sold and the revenue from the transaction was either reinvested in the remaining properties or spent on operations of the HNFR.

The Hunguest Corporation, enjoying a 20-year exclusive property management contract for the properties, set up individual public limited (management) companies for every hotel. The hotels were managed as part of the Hunguest Hotels chain. In 1997, the board of HNFR accepted the proposal of Hunguest Corporation that each property should be transferred into the individual public limited companies in which the Hunguest Corporation acquires majority stake. This step also made Hunguest property available for private investors. Later, a new investor initiated raising capital in the individual companies which prepared the way for the gradual takeover of the company, since Hunguest Corporation was unable to raise sufficient funds to secure their own ownership.

Since 1992, the whole takeover process has been criticised by politicians and trade union officials, among others. The major argument is that the agreements between the Foundation, the Hunguest Corporation Trust and the individual companies were not adequately negotiated. This left the transactions arguable and open to bribing or money-laundering assumptions, especially considering that the Government provided the HNFR with approximately 13 million EUR between 1992 and 1998.

The current Hungarian HCS

The HCS was introduced in 1998 by the HNFR as the exclusive holiday cheque issuer, manager and distributor.

The HCS has the official responsibility to provide support for selected social groups, i.e. employees with low income, people with social disadvantages; pensioners and students. Until January 2010, the Taxation Law ensures tax exemption for both the buyers, i.e. employers (who do not have to pay employment tax on the amount given in the form of holiday cheques), as well as for the beneficiaries, i.e. members of privileged social groups (who do not pay personal income tax on the amount received as holiday cheques), unless the value of the cheque exceeded the actual minimum salary, 71,500 HUF/month in 2009 (approximately 264 EUR at the exchange rate valid in August 2009).

The HCS provides the users with the opportunity to decide where and which services they would like to use from the range of services available. The beneficiaries can be classi- fied into two groups: indigent persons, e.g. children living in low-income families, students, the unemployed, pensioners and other disadvantaged groups, and employees, since employers can also allocate holiday cheques for their workers as a tax-free incentive.

Consequently, among the possible buyers of holiday cheques there are private companies, i.e. corporations and other companies providing support for employees and family members; public sector organisations that are financed from the central budget, and local governments for public and civil servants and for their relatives, and the HNFR.

The HCS provides two ways in which one can acquire the cheques: employers can buy the cheques from HNFR for the employees, and the other beneficiary groups, such as retired people or the unemployed can apply themselves for support to HNFR. The purchase of the cheques is generally a straightforward process. Employers, according to their human resource policies and tax-optimisation strategies, can buy the cheques both for the employees and their relatives, up to the maximum amount. However, for those who are not employed and are entitled to receive holiday cheques due to their disadvantaged socio-economic situation, the process is a little more complicated. The Board of HNFR decides every year the allocation of the available funding among the disadvantaged groups. This is not an easy process since the number of eligible applicants is always much higher than the funds available. This subsidy reaches the people concerned through an open application process. The selection is based on normative criteria, e.g. per capita income, family status, family size, student status and retired status – those who meet these criteria are automatically eligible. The HNFR is in co-operation with 150 organisations all around the country that inform applicants and assist them with the application process.

Socially disadvantaged individuals can apply for cheques in the framework of an application programme announced by the HNFR every year. The programme is open for individuals in four categories:

- Pensioners.
- Individuals living with disability.
- Students in skilled (blue-collar) worker education.
- Employed people who raise more than one child.

So far, the business sector has played the most important role in the operation of the HCS. In 2008, 75% of all cheques were purchased by the business sector (Figure 4). The main reason why private companies favour holidays cheques to other financial incentives is that they can provide their employees (and their relatives) with a higher tax-free income. Certainly, extra payment in the form of holiday cheques is a restricted kind of income, since it can only be spent at certain places and for certain services: unless the cheques are actually used, the increase may be considered only a virtual revenue.

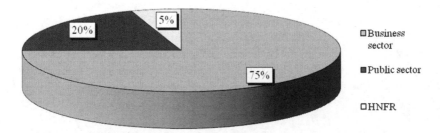

Figure 4.   Distribution of holiday cheque buyers (2008).

However, since Hungary has one of the highest tax-burdens on employment in the European Union, private companies look for ways in which they can increase salaries, but do not increase associated tax expenses.

In the past 3 years, the Foundation contributed to the improvement of the quality of life of more than 350,000 socially disadvantaged people through the HCS.

In 2008, the HNFR accumulated approximately €8.5 million from three major sources:

- Charitable partner organisations and civil groups that provide support for those potential beneficiaries who qualify for holiday cheques but are unable to cover even the minimum expected self-contribution (€3 million).
- Dividend from Hunguest Corporation and Hunguest Hotels (€1.4 million).
- Income from the cheques purchased (€4.1 million).

During 2008, in the framework of the application programmes for disadvantaged social groups, the HNFR gave support to 64.500 applicants worth €8.8 million, which means an average of €136 per person.

Use of the cheques

Every holiday cheque is registered, they can be used only for domestic services and they cannot be exchanged into cash. In this way, the HNFR can ensure that all beneficiaries spend their additional income in the Hungarian tourism and leisure market. Equally importantly, it is expected that the cheques will be spent on leisure and tourism experiences, cultural development and relaxation, among others.

Since the holiday cheques were in principle successors of the socialist trade union issued-vouchers, originally the use of cheques was limited for the accommodation sector, i.e. participants had very limited freedom in their consumption choices. Table 2 presents the gradual expansion of the possible use of cheques between 1998 and 2009.

The proliferation of possible uses made the government a little suspicious. Since more and more leisure- and recreation-related services became available through the HCS, the system started to offer opportunities for a limited – but nationally significant – level of corporate tax evasion, while the lack of focus on tourism services decreased the system's efficiency in domestic tourism development. Interestingly, in the very beginning, the name of the HNFR was not really accurate, since the original objective was to provide support for domestic holidays away from home: however, in 2009, the activities and the name are in harmony, since today the NHFR provides support for recreation.

As Figure 5 presents though, of the many possible ways of spending the cheques, travellers still tend to prefer accommodation services.

The spatial distribution of holiday cheque demand reflects the development patterns of the Hungarian tourism industry as well. Although the regional figures present a relatively homogenous distribution (Figure 6), the most popular destinations where beneficiaries spend their cheques are the capital city, Budapest, and the Lake Balaton region, as well as spa towns all around the country and mountain resorts in the north-eastern region.

Along with the extension of the possible uses, the number of services where these cheques are accepted was growing gradually in the period of 1998–2004, and expanded significantly since 2005, as companies discovered the potential of attracting new segments and increasing their revenue in the slightly less volatile domestic market. By 2009, approximately 10,000 partners redeemed the cheques all around the country (Figure 7). The partner companies are generally satisfied with the system: in a recent study, their

Table 2.   The expansion of the range of services covered by holiday cheques in Hungary, 1998–2009.

1998–2003	2004–2006	2007–2008	2009
Accommodation	Accommodation	Accommodation	Accommodation
	Eating out	Eating out	Catering/eating out
	Fishing permits	Fishing permits	Fishing permits
	Cultural programs, festivals, zoo	Cultural programs, festivals, zoo	(in a new category)
	Fuel	Fuel	N/A
	Travelling by train, coach and ship	Travelling by train, coach and ship	Travelling by train, coach and ship
	Visiting thermal baths	Visiting thermal baths	Visiting thermal baths
		Cultural attractions, sightseeing	Visiting zoos and botanical gardens
		Health conservation and illness prevention	Cultural services
		Leisure sports (e.g. fitness, wellness)	Health conservation and illness prevention
			Swimming pool services and spa treatment
			Sport-and cultural services (including Formula-1, and BNV Exhibition Centre)
			Renting equipment
			Pleasure flights
			Motorway tickets
			Cinema tickets
			Internet subscription
			Domestic travel insurance

Source: HNFR 2009, www.mnua.hu.

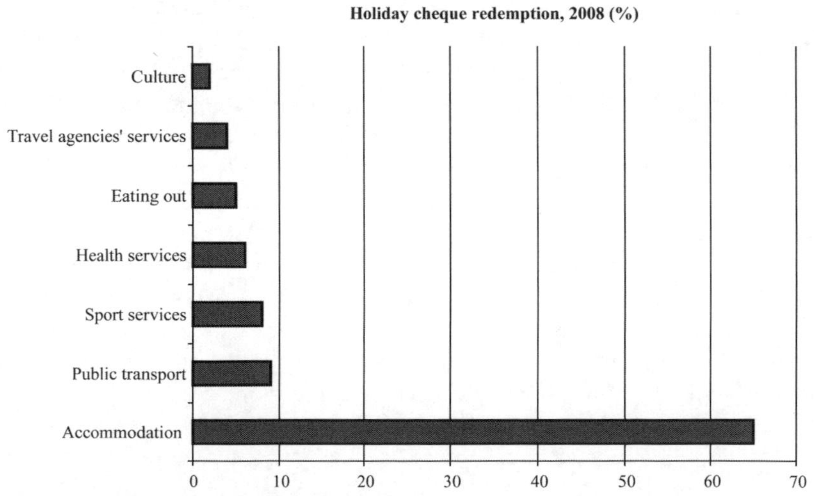

Figure 5.   Holiday cheque redemption, 2008 (%).
Source: www.mnua.hu.

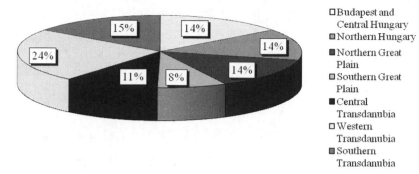

Legend:
□ Budapest and Central Hungary
▣ Northern Hungary
■ Northern Great Plain
□ Southern Great Plain
■ Central Transdanubia
□ Western Transdanubia
▣ Southern Transdanubia

Figure 6.   The spatial distribution of holiday cheque demand, 2008.
Source: UP IG, 2008.

level of satisfaction reached 7.68 (on a 1–10 Likert scale with 10 being most satisfied) (UP IG, 2008). Partner companies assume an even higher satisfaction level if the perceived value of guest satisfaction was considered, i.e. 8.39. The lower satisfaction level of partner companies is mainly related to administrative difficulties and the amount of partnership fee which can be too high for smaller companies.

The popularity of using the cheque can be represented by the turnover generated, which increased by nearly 15 times between 2000 and 2007 (Figure 8). In the year 2007, social tourism generated a turnover of almost €125 million (approximately 30 billion HUF). Demand for state-supported travel has also been growing (from 2006 to 2007, a 45% rise can be observed, due to the widening range of services available within the system, and the increasing acknowledgement of the financial benefits of using holiday cheques). However, only 3% of all holiday cheque users qualified for the financial support due to their disadvantaged social status, which is a significant change compared to 2006 when nearly 30% of the holiday cheque owners were socially indigent.

A similar tendency can be observed in the number of the cheque users (Figure 9). In 2000, there were only around 100,000 individual beneficiaries, while by 2008, this number increased to 900,000, with approximately €145 financial support for each

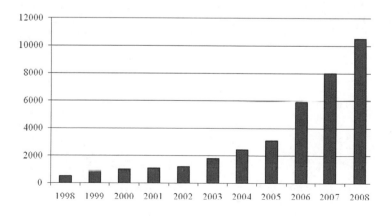

Figure 7.   Number of contracted partners, 1998–2008.
Source: www.mnua.hu.

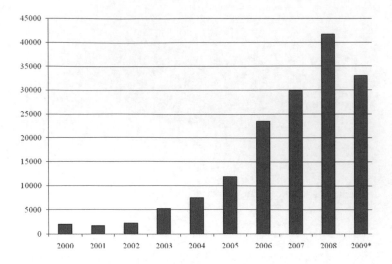

Figure 8.   Turnover generated by holiday cheques between 2000 and 2009 (billion HUF).
Source: www.mnua.hu. *Preliminary figure.

person, resulting in a total budget of €9.12 million. In 2008, only 64,459 socially disadvantaged individuals received cheques from the HNFR, i.e. the vast majority of cheque users
are employees whose employers provide them with the holiday cheques as a specific form
of remuneration. According to a research carried out by the Institute of Geography at the
University of Pécs, over 86% of holiday cheque beneficiaries have at least average – or
higher – income (UP IG, 2008), which highlights the system's limited ability to involve
the truly unprivileged social groups.
        In order to further increase the popularity of the HCS, in January 2008, the HNFR intro-
duced a new programme called Holiday Cheque Plus Sale, which is open for those service
providers who offer something extra in addition to their basic services (e.g. welcome drink,

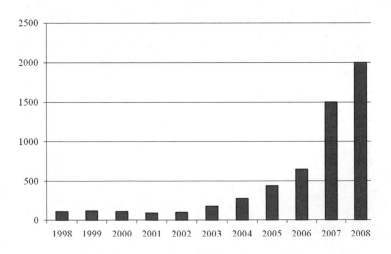

Figure 9.   Number of holiday cheque beneficiaries between 1998 and 2008.

spa ticket or other complementary service) to those guests who pay with holiday cheques as opposed to cash. Unfortunately, there is no statistical information available on the outcome of this project.

The present and the future of social tourism in Hungary

As mentioned earlier, there is no separate infrastructure for 'social tourism' in Hungary – as opposed to the network of trade union-owned accommodation establishments of the socialist era or to the current French system of holiday villages. Today holiday cheques are accepted by a great variety of service providers who are contracted partners of the HNFR. Together with the allocation system of holiday cheques, this results in a situation where the state subsidises the tourism and recreation consumption of a wide range of social segments, and not exclusively the most disadvantaged socio-economic groups.

As discussed earlier, today the amount of holiday cheques received is 100% tax-free up to the value of the current minimum salary, the amount of which is set by the government (71,500 HUF, i.e. €288 in August 2009). This will evidently change: due to the global economic recession, and partially due to the shift from the original objectives to the proliferation of uses, the Hungarian Parliament accepted certain changes which came into effect on 1 January 2010. The most important change is that employers have to pay 25% over every HUF they give to their employees in the form of holiday cheque, up to the value of the minimum wage. Should they wish to give more, 54% tax is payable on the amount exceeding the minimum wage. Obviously, this planned measure met the opposition of the Hungarian tourism industry, since preliminary forecasts suggest that the transformation of the system will significantly affect the willingness of companies to offer holiday cheques to their employees. Although the decision is in harmony with the greater efforts of the government to mitigate the impacts of the global economic crisis and to decrease central budget expenses, the measure will most probably influence domestic tourism demand unfavourably. At a time when most neighbouring countries bring about opposite measures to stimulate domestic travel, e.g. the Romanian government urgently introduced a HCS in early 2009, the transformation of the Hungarian system does not seem to strengthen the country's competitiveness within the Central Eastern European tourism market.

Decreasing domestic demand in a country where approximately 50% of all guest nights registered at commercial accommodation services are spent by domestic guests will certainly have a negative impact on many tourism companies' profitability, most probably leading to cost cuts, lay-offs and a generally declining service quality level. According to the forecast of the Hotel Association of Hungary, domestic demand may drop by up to 30% which may result in drastic price wars among hotels to increase their popularity and consequent bankruptcies in the sector, together with an increase in illegal employment. A recent research by K&H Bank (VG Online, 2009) revealed that 15% of companies would already consider dropping some supported means of benefits from the cafeteria systems (a flexible system of employee benefits where employees can choose from different types of fringe benefit elements and receive customised packages) and only 20% would keep holiday cheques.

Although these arguments are all valid and relevant, it should be noted that they are all related to the positive economic impacts of the HCS such as employment, income or tax revenue, and the social principles of welfare tourism systems, e.g. solidarity or social inclusion, are rather neglected compared to the economic benefits. This may partly be related to the global economic crisis and the fact that Hungary has been one of the worst affected economies in Europe, but also to the general disposition of the Hungarian society and decision-makers. Quantified economic benefits are generally seen as much stronger arguments than qualitative advantages It may also be assumed that although the right to rest is a generally accepted human right, holidays are still seen as some sort of luxury by certain segments of the Hungarian society who may question the necessity of supporting others peoples' holidays by the state.

The future of social tourism and particularly that of the currently successful HCS are rather uncertain today. There is a wide range of economic and social interests and expectations related to the transformation of the system. Companies wish to find the most cost-effective ways of employee remuneration, domestic tourism businesses want to maintain, or preferably increase, domestic demand, leisure and recreation services wish the HNFR to widen the range of services available within the HCS. The government aims to decrease central expenses and increase tax revenues, and ordinary citizens expect to receive financial support for their well-deserved holidays. Hopefully, in the coming years, decision-makers will recognise the benefits of a well-established social tourism system, and future transformation measures will improve the system's effectiveness and efficiency.

Note

1. At the time, both of the authors worked at the TRC and were involved in the above-mentioned project.

References

Allcock, J.B., & Przeclawski, K. (1990). Introduction. *Annals of Tourism Research, 17*(1), 1–6.

Bhatia, A.A. (2006). *The business of tourism: Concepts and strategies.* New Delhi: Sterling Publishers Private Limited.

EESC. (2006). *Opinion of the European Economic and Social Committee on Social Tourism in Europe.* Retrieved August 26, 2009, from http://eur-lex.europa.eu/LexUriServ/LexUriServ.do?uri=OJ:C:2006:318:0067:0077:EN:PDF.

Higgins-Desbiolles, F. (2006). More than an 'industry': The forgotten power of tourism as a social force. *Tourism Management, 27*(6), 1192–1208.

HNFR. (2008). *The Recreation Cheque System in Hungary.* Retrieved August 25, 2009, from http://www.mnua.hu/pdf/20081023angol.pdf.

HNFR. (2009). *Általános információ.* Retrieved August 25, 2009, from http://www.udulesicsekk.hu/index.php?q=felhasznaloknak.

Hungarian National Tourist Office. (2009). *Tourism in Hungary 2008.* Budapest: Hungarian National Tourist Office.

Jordan, P. (2006). Tourism and EU enlargement: A Central European perspective. In D. Hall, M. Smith, & B. Marciszewska (Eds.), *Tourism in the new Europe: The challenges and opportunities of EU enlargement* (pp. 65–80). Wallingford: CAB International.

Lengyel, M. (1998). Az Európai Unióhoz való csatlakozásra készülő közép-európai országok turizmusa [Tourism in CEE Countries Preparing to Join the EU]. *Turizmus Bulletin, 2*(2), 24–39.

Lengyel, M., Puczkó, L., & Rátz, T. (1996). *A szociálturizmusban kidolgozandó 'Üdültetési Csekk'-rendszer bevezetése, várható hatásai, eredményei [The Introduction, Expected Impacts and Results of the Establishment of a 'Holiday Cheque' System in Social Tourism],* (Unpublished Research Report). Budapest: Budapest University of Economic Sciences, Tourism Research Centre.

Michalkó, G. (2007). *A turizmuselmélet alapjai [Principles of Tourism].* Székesfehérvár: Kodolányi János Főiskola.

Minnaert, L. (2007). *Social Tourism: A Potential Policy to Reduce Social Exclusion?* Paper presented at the UTSG Annual Conference, Leeds.

Pohner, T. (2008). *A rendszerváltozások hatása Magyarország turizmusára [The Impacts of Political Changes on Hungarian Tourism]*. Retrieved August 25, 2009, from http://elib.kkf.hu/okt_publ/szf_23_13.pdf.

Poy, C. (2003). *Les atouts du tourisme social*. Retrieved August 23, from http://www.humanite.fr/2003-07-29_Societe_Les-atouts-du-tourisme-social.

Puczkó, L., & Rátz, T. (2006). Product development and diversification in Hungary. In D. Hall, M. Smith, & B. Marciszewska (Eds.), *Tourism in the new Europe: The challenges and opportunities of EU enlargement* (pp. 116–126). Wallingford: CAB International.

Rátz, T. (1996). Privatisation in the Hungarian tourism industry. In A. Rapacz (Ed.), *Aktualne Problemy Ekonomiczne i Prawno-organizacyjne Gospodarki Turystycznej w Europie* (pp. 156–163). Wroclaw: Wydawnictwo Akademii Ekonomicznej im. Oskara Langego we Wroclawiu.

Ryan, C. (2002). Equity, management, power sharing and sustainability – issues of the 'new tourism'. *Tourism Management, 23*(1), 17–26.

Spode, H. (2004). Fordism, mass tourism and the third reich: The 'Strength through Joy' seaside resort as an index fossil. *Journal of Social History, 38*(1), 127–155.

State Audit Office. (2001). *ÁSZ jelentés az MNÜA tevékenységéről [State Audit Office Report on the Activity of the HNFR]*. Budapest: State Audit Office.

UP IG. (2008). *Az üdülési csekk forgalmazásának az életminőségre gyakorolt hatása helyi és regionális dimenziókban: kutatási jelentés [Research Report: Local and Regional Dimensions of the Impacts of the Holiday Cheque System on Quality of Life]*. Pécs: University of Pécs, Institute of Geography.

VG Online. (2009). *Étkezési jegy, üdülési csekk – Mire hajlandóak a cégek? [Catering tickets, holiday cheques – What are companies ready to use?]*. Retrieved August 17, 2009, from http://www.vg.hu/nyomtat.php?cikk=285187.

WTO. (1980). *Manila Declaration on World Tourism*. Retrieved August 23, 2009, from http://www.univeur.org/CMS/UserFiles/65.%20Manila.PDF.

Away from daily routines – holiday as a societal norm and a manifestation of an unequal society

Minna Ylikännö

Social Insurance Institution of Finland, Peltolantie 3, FI-20720 Turku

Introduction

Holidaying can be dismissed lightly as a frivolous and hedonistic pursuit, something that people may enjoy in their lives like expensive designer clothing or jewellery. Consequently, the inability to engage in tourism activities is not necessary perceived as something that would affect people's state of mind significantly, or could be seen as excluding them from society. However, it has been shown that holidays can play a central role in people's well-being. They may significantly increase social and family capital for the participants and, especially among low-income groups, the benefits of tourism can be high (Minnaert & Schapmans, 2009). Hence, enabling an occasional holiday away from home could be seen as an investment in the well-being of society (see Hughes, 1991; Quinn & Stacey, 2010). Having a one-week annual holiday away from home on yearly is considered important to individuals' well-being in some societies, and can be included in indices used to measure material deprivation. For example in the EU, material deprivation indicators are based on nine items including 'one-week annual holiday away from home' (Fusco et al., 2011; see also Halleröd et al., 2006; Nolan & Whelan, 2010).

From a time use perspective, a holiday away from home is considered a valuable interruption of clock time and of daily routines. Furthermore, it gives a possibility to leave problems behind for a few days, to rest and relax, and to spend time with family (Minnaert & Schapmans 2009, p. 53). Rising real incomes in some parts of the world and some segments of the population have combined with technical changes such as the growth of the internet and changing business models such as the advent of low cost carriers have combined to promote domestic and overseas tourist destinations, and in many regions of the world the tourism sector continues to expand at a rapid pace and increasing numbers of people are travelling away from home for a holiday, with some taking more than one holiday per year (Nawijn et al., 2010, p. 36).

As a result, rather than being a luxury, it can be argued that holidays are an essential part of contemporary life in affluent societies (Smith & Hughes, 1999, p. 124). From this perspective, those not able to holiday away from home, because of financial pressures, are to a certain degree socially excluded. According to the definition of the Commission of the European Communities (1993), social exclusion refers, among other things, to suffering from low self-esteem and stigmatisation (see also Rodgers, 1995). In other words, we feel ourselves less worthy when unable to participate in the commonly accepted style of life of the community (Dawson, 1988; Richards, 1998). Therefore enabling holidays can be seen as a potential means to promote and encourage equality and social inclusion (Minnaert et al., 2006).

One way to counter social exclusion is to offer social holidays for disadvantaged groups. In the countries that promote social tourism, there is usually an ethical notion that the weaker strata should be given the opportunity to raise their life to an acceptable standard through participating in the tourism industry. Further, holidaying is seen as a necessity without which the risk of social exclusion increases (Minnaert et al., 2006.) Obviously, not all countries share the ethical foundation that all its members should be offered the possibility of an annual holiday away from home. The different views with regards to holidaying are manifested in national policies. In some countries social tourism is an integral part of policies intended to combat social exclusion. In other countries alternative measures are seen as more important, and social tourism is either left to charitable organisations to arrange or does not exist as such.

In this chapter the focus is not on social tourism *per se*, but on the meaning of a holiday on a more general level. It argues that those who are able to live up to norms prevailing in society at a given time, in this case have a holiday away from home once a year, feel more respected by their peers, which in turn reflects their perceived position in the social strata. This chapter will investigate the relationship between holidaying away from home and the individual's subjective feeling of social status and argue that there is a relationship that persists even when controlling for individual characteristics such as age, gender, income and labour market status as well as for the country of residence. In other words, the chapter will examine whether holidays are regarded an integral part of contemporary life, in which case non-participation in holidays not only increases the risk of social exclusion, but also leads to a reduction in perceived social status. Individuals perceive social status in relation to others in society. By analysing quantitative, internationally comparative data, the chapter will examine the effect of holiday participation on social status. If holiday participation is shown to be a measure of exclusion, then perhaps it should not be dismissed as frivolous, but considered an investment not only in the well-being of individuals but also in the social cohesion.

Holidaying as a socially accepted and expected way of using time

Holidays are often considered as an extended period of time away from paid work: productive, hardworking people need an extended period of time to recover from work. When annual paid leave systems were introduced, the intention was to provide employees with a period of rest and recovery. France was the first country in Europe to introduce paid annual holidays, in 1936; since then entitlements to paid leave have become common in affluent societies, and may extend to four to five weeks annually. Today, employees in the EU with full-time contracts have typically the right to 20–30 annual paid leave days. However, by defining holidays as an opposite to paid work we implicitly exclude many groups who are in unpaid work or not working, such as carers, househusbands and housewives, the unemployed and pensioners. These groups do not need a break from paid work, but nevertheless they may be in need for *a break from daily routines*, from the non-paid work. Haukeland (1990) found that most people, regardless of their labour market status, have the need to travel occasionally away from home during holidays in order to break away from the monotony of everyday life with obligations and routines. According to Clarke and Critcher (1985, p. 88), '[a holiday] is a special sort of time. If not actually timeless, holidays replace the rhythms of paid work *and domestic work* obligations with potential choice over the use of time.' Hence, holidaying appears equally important for both those in paid labour and those whose daily routines consist of housework, care for children or other family members, and other non-paid work – and those who are not working at all. Hence, if we think of a holiday as time away from daily routines it is important to non-workers as well as those in paid employment.

Holidaying away from the home is only one way among others to use the spare time that people have. However, the results from a series of studies show that people perceive holidaying more than just merely a way of spending time. Not only those who have made a holiday trip but also those who are waiting to go on a holiday are happier and more satisfied with their life. Moreover, the positive memories generated from the holiday trips contribute to satisfaction in many aspects of life domains, not only in leisure time (see for example Smith and Hughes, 1999; Gilbert and Abdullah, 2002; Minnaert, 2007; Minnaert & Schapmans, 2009; Sirgy et al., 2011).

Holidays that are offered for those who could not otherwise afford a holiday away from home through social tourism are shown to have a particularly positive effect on various aspects of daily life. For example, participation in social tourism led to greater self-confidence and participants felt mentally stronger after a holiday (Minnaert & Schapmans, 2009, p. 59.) and for families from low-income groups participation in social holidays could lead to an increase in family capital: the relationships between the family members and their resilience when faced with adversity (Minnaert et al., 2006, p. 30).

On the other hand, Nawijn (2010) did not find any long-term positive effects of vacationing on happiness or life-satisfaction. The positive effects that vacationing has are, according to Nawijn (2010) and Nawijn et al. (2010), limited to the duration of the holiday trip itself and to a brief phase of anticipation and afterglow. Also, not all holiday trips turn out to be pleasant breaks from daily routines. Some people suffer from jet lag, homesickness, worries about crime, relationship problems, and different kinds of health problems (Nawijn, 2010). They constitute a small minority of all travellers, however, and generally people feel good during their holiday trips (Nawijn, 2010). Despite this view that holiday trips create only short-term, temporary states of happiness with no long-term life-improving impact (Nawijn, 2010; Nawijn et al., 2010), most commentators consider holidays important to well-being. Among other things they have found to ensure more dignity and improve enjoyment of life through the ability to participate in the society (see e.g. Haulot, 1981; Minnaert & Schapmans, 2009). Urry (1990, p. 4) compares holidaying to possessing a car or a nice house: 'It is a matter of status in modernist societies.' From this viewpoint, holidaying cannot be regarded as just a way to spend the spare time but rather as an indicator of well-being and social fabric (Hughes 1991). When Urry made this argument in 1990 there were slightly over 400 million tourist arrivals. In 2009, just two decades later, the corresponding figure had risen to 880 million. Approximately half of these were travel for leisure, recreation and holiday. Increasing numbers of people are travelling away from home for a holiday. Even if authors disagree about the benefits of holidaying, it is clear that holidays have become a common – for many, a routine – aspect of modern life.

Social exclusion and subjective social status

Those with little money, with care commitments, or with disabilities are often those who most desire occasional escape from their daily routines. However, at the same time they may find it very difficult to take advantage of the opportunities offered by the tourism industry because of financial or other pressures (Richards, 1998). Not surprisingly, financial constraints are one major reason for not taking a holiday away from home (see Hughes,

1991; Mergoupis & Steuer, 2003). Travel to and accommodation at the holiday destination must be paid for, and money is also needed for recreation. For those from lower income groups even a small investment for a modest holiday such as a camping trip or a weekend in a holiday village may turn out to be unaffordable; some people do not have the chance to travel away from home even for a short holiday. This situation is exacerbated by the fact that in affluent societies, where large proportions of the population participate in holidays, it has almost become a form of social exclusion not to do so. From this point of view, holidaying is not just about short-term benefits and about happiness; rather, as a socially accepted way of using time, it is a matter of status (see e.g. Urry 1990). Such an argument clearly needs justification. Previous research on the relationship between relative deprivation, poverty and subjective social status has indicated that when assessing social status, we should not focus only on income or on material circumstances. Whilst these play a crucial role in individuals' self-assessment, there are other drivers as well, such as family relationships, health status, and educational achievements (Batty & Flint, 2010). There is evidence that living on low incomes generate low self-esteem (Batty & Flint, 2010, p. 46), which is further linked to the individuals' subjective assessment of themselves (see Lindemann, 2007). Why are income or material possessions so important for self-assessment and self-esteem? Sen (1999) argues that poor people are ashamed of being unable to realise the basic capabilities consistent with the society in which they live. Furthermore, when people are ashamed of being poor, they compare themselves to those in a better position in the society. Subjective social position depends thus not only on objective characteristics such as income levels or educational achievements but also on how people experience their place in society and their position in comparison to others – as well as what they imagine their position to be in the future. In other words, people assess themselves by reference to the people around them – their reference group (Lindemann, 2007). If having a holiday away from home once or twice a year is expected in one's reference group, those who have to forego holiday trips would, according to Sen (1999) feel ashamed of their situation. This can be self-reinforcing: when they become aware of their lower position in the stratification system, they are likely to locate themselves yet further down in the social strata. The reference group individuals compare themselves within when it comes to holidaying is thus of the utmost importance. According to Evans and Kelley (2004), the sampling of reference persons is to certain extent highly subjective: 'It is as if each respondent mentally draws a sample of people in their own social world – a sample of their family, friends, and co-workers – and derives their picture of society from that small and biased sample. That is why people's perception of their social position tends to be pushed towards the middle, meaning that people place a large number of people both above and under themselves on the social strata' (see also Lindemann, 2007). Respondents want to be average in their own social world and are thus reluctant to choose extremes on numeric scales measuring social status (Evans & Kelley, 2004). However, at the same time, social stratification pulls people apart, away from the middle strata (Evans and Kelley, 2004, p. 7). Hence, those who cannot afford a holiday away from home may locate themselves lower down on the numeric scales of subjective social status rather than 'stick' to the middle as a result.

Data and methods

This study analyses data from the International Social Survey Programme (ISSP) 2007 with a focus on leisure time and sports. The ISSP is a continuing annual programme of cross-national collaboration on surveys covering topics important for social science research. The first ISSP was conducted in 1985 with a focus on the role of the government. Since then national data have been collected on a yearly basis and merged into one cross-national database. Topics vary annually, but some modules have been replicated one or more times. A survey focusing on leisure and sports has been conducted only in 2007.

The ISSP surveys are conducted by interview and post. Most surveys begin with interviews with a stratified random sample followed by a leave-behind self-completion questionnaire containing the ISSP items. Some surveys are conducted entirely by post and some entirely by interview (Evans & Kelley, 2004). The 2007 Leisure and Sports module contains a number of questions on leisure time activities, the meaning of spare time and leisure in relation to work and other spheres of life, and social determinants and consequences of leisure. It also contains questions on sport/game activities but since the focus in this study is on holidaying, sport-related questions are excluded.

The 2007 survey covers 34 countries from Europe, Asia, Australia, North America and South America. Since the focus of this chapter is on holidaying away from home as an integral part of contemporary life in modern affluent societies, and on the consequences of non-travel for social status, a group of wealthy countries have been selected for study. The ten wealthiest countries in terms of GDP per capita (in year 2007) that included a question on subjective social status in their questionnaire have been selected from the original 34 countries in ISSP 2007. These countries are in alphabetical order Australia, Belgium, Finland, France, Germany, Ireland, Japan, Norway, Sweden, and Switzerland. Unfortunately, some wealthy countries such as the USA and the UK had to be excluded because they had not included the question on subjective social status in their questionnaire.

All respondents between the ages 15 and 98 are included in the study. The median age in the data is 48 and 90 per cent of the respondents are between the ages of 21 and 77. Just under half of the respondents (45 per cent) are working full-time, 12 per cent are working part-time, 21 per cent are retired, and the rest are not participating in the labour market for other reasons. In the final data, the number of respondents per country varies from a little over 1,000 to almost 2,800. In total there are 15,915 respondents in the final data.

Respondents were asked where they would put themselves on a scale measuring social position in the society. They could choose between 1 and 10. Respondents generally answered the question, with missing data averaging 6.4 per cent overall. Missing data was however not equally distributed between the countries. Belgians were the most likely and Australians the least likely to answer the question, with rates of missing data of 0.8 per cent and 13.0 per cent, respectively. Moreover, there were individual differences between the respondents according to gender, age and education. Men were a little more likely to answer the question than women. On the other hand, older people and those with lower education were less likely to answer the question.

Respondents were also asked how many nights altogether they had stayed away from home for holidays or social visits within the last 12 months. They could choose between (1) I was not away, (2) 1–5 nights, (3) 6–10 nights, (4) 11–20 nights, (5) 21–30 nights, and (6) more than 30 nights. In the descriptive analysis the original variable with a 6-point scale is used. For multivariate analysis the original variable is recoded into a binary variable with 0 representing non-travellers and 1 those who spent at least one night away from home on holiday. From the respondents, 17 per cent had not been any nights away from home for a holiday within the past 12 months, 30 per cent had travelled away from home for 1–10 nights and 52 per cent more than 10 nights.

Other independent variables are age (continuous), gender (1 = male), education (in years), status on the labour market (1 = employed full-time), marital status (1 = married), household composition (1 = family with children), subjective health (1 = good, very good or excellent), lack of money (1 = very much or to a large extent), and lack of time (1 = very much or to a large extent). The last two variables measure the extent to which these conditions prevent the respondents from engaging in the free-time activities they would like. The ISSP 2007 data also includes objective variables for individual and household income. For this study, a subjective measure was chosen as it describes the financial security of the family better than the objective variables that do not take household and individual differences in financial adequacy into account. Lack of time was included in the model to control the impact of long working hours to social status.

The chapter first focuses on distributions and means of subjective social status identifications and the central tendency of these distributions for each of the ten countries. Then it examines these distributions and means separately for each of the six groups (the total number of nights the respondent stayed away from home for holidays) of non-travellers and travellers. After the descriptive analysis it assesses the impact of individual level variables and national context on social status via linear regression analysis. Linear regression is chosen because it is assumed that respondents, when answering the question on social status, think of the response scale in numerical terms, considering distances as equal. In addition, the use of linear regression models in this case is justified, as the subjective social status variable has a relatively large number of categories (ten). Thus the measure of subjective social status can be treated as a continuous variable. The assumption of equal distances is critical because if it is assumed that the different social strata do not represent equal intervals on an underlying social hierarchy, another estimation procedure, such as a logit or probit model, should be applied (see Evans & Kelley, 2004).

Results

As discussed above, it can be argued that those who cannot afford to holiday away from home annually are at risk of deprivation and social exclusion and do not benefit in well-being from having an occasional break from daily routines. Most research done in holidaying and especially in the benefits of holidaying is qualitative and subjective in nature. Holiday-makers are typically asked after having a holiday about their experiences of holidaying away from home after which the researchers have differentiated its short- and long-term effects on their well-being. Further, the existing research covering the well-being aspect concentrates mostly on social tourism and not on holidaying on the more general level.

The results from previous studies show more positive than negative effects of holidaying (see e.g. Minnaert & Schapmans, 2009; Sirgy et al., 2011). This is to be expected since the very idea of holidaying revolves around seeking pleasure and enjoyment. Only when expectations of the holiday are not met or a misfortune such as illness occurs do people experience their recent holiday less positively. Despite possible risks for something negative to happen, most of us look forward to travelling away from home for a holiday.

However, there is a lack of comparative studies, which could give a more comprehensive picture of the meaning holidaying away from home has for people and the effects of exclusion from holidaying. Nationally representative, and in this case often qualitative, studies are valuable in understanding holidaying away from home as a mechanism of social inclusion. However, large studies with quantitative data covering several countries are needed to reveal the mechanisms behind well-being and holidaying. The ISSP survey is a large-scale quantitative study that can be used to investigate the relationship between holidaying away from home and the individual's subjective feeling of social status – and how far people feel less worthy in society if they are excluded from holidaying.

First, the relationship between holidaying and subjective social status is assessed by examining the distributions of different groups of travellers into social strata. Table 1 shows that subjective assessment of social status increases as the number of holidays away from home increases. In fact, there appears to be a linear relationship between holidaying and subjective social status. Although most respondents chose the middle strata, the group means show that the more people holiday away from home the higher they locate themselves in the social strata. While 19 per cent of the non-travellers locate themselves in the three lowest strata, among those who holiday away from home for more than 30 nights per year only 5 per cent locate themselves in those strata. On the other hand, among the non-travellers only 8 per cent locate themselves in the three highest strata compared to the most frequent travellers, where the corresponding share is as high as 20 per cent.

Table 1   Distributions of subjective social status by number of holidays and country

Subjective social status: Percentage in each stratum												
	1	2	3	4	5	6	7	8	9	10	N	Mean
I was not away	4	4	11	14	26	23	10	6	1	1	2432	5.1
1–5 nights	2	4	9	14	24	24	14	7	1	1	2262	5.4
6–10 nights	1	2	7	10	26	27	17	8	2	1	2183	5.6
11–20 nights	1	2	5	10	21	26	22	11	2	1	2989	5.9
21–30 nights	1	1	4	8	19	28	24	13	2	1	1980	6.1
More than 30 nights	1	1	3	6	18	27	24	16	3	1	2722	6.2

	1	2	3	4	5	6	7	8	9	10	N	Mean	% of non-travellers
Australia	1	1	4	7	20	19	22	12	2	1	2408	6.1	15
Belgium	0	1	3	6	30	24	25	8	2	1	1247	6.0	24
Finland	2	2	6	10	22	18	19	14	2	1	1287	5.8	8
France	3	4	8	15	17	29	12	5	1	0	1906	5.2	10
Germany	1	3	7	10	15	32	16	9	2	1	1641	5.7	32
Ireland	1	1	6	11	32	18	13	6	2	0	1849	5.5	22
Japan	2	4	15	18	28	18	9	3	1	0	1220	4.8	26
Norway	1	1	3	4	8	32	22	19	4	2	1110	6.5	6
Sweden	2	2	4	6	10	36	21	12	2	2	1249	6.1	13
Switzerland	2	3	7	10	23	22	19	10	2	1	977	5.6	14

Note: Cells with 10 per cent or more are shaded.
Source: ISSP 2007<AQ14>

The difference between the groups in the subjective social status is clear. The non-travellers, whether voluntary or non-voluntary, perceive their social status not only as significantly lower than those who travel a lot, but also as lower than those who made only a short trip within the last 12 months. Hence, it is clear that not being able to travel away from home for a holiday is linked to subjective social status.

Table 1 also shows the distribution of subjective social status in the ten wealthy countries chosen for this study. Most people see themselves as located in the higher rather than the lower strata. In all countries except for Japan most people locate themselves in stratum 5, 6 or 7. In Norway subjective social status is the highest, with on average 25 per cent of the respondents locating themselves in the three highest strata and only 17 per cent in strata 1–5. The mean for social status is 6.5 in Norway and only 4.8 in Japan, which has, on average, the lowest subjective social status among the respondents. In Japan 4 per cent of the respondents locate themselves in the three highest strata whereas 67 per cent of the respondents see themselves as located in strata 1–5.

As all ten countries are wealthy and rank high in terms of income equality, we might expect a more equal distribution of subjective social status between them (see Evans & Kelley, 2004), but there are clear differences in the distributions of social status. Differences in the share of non-travellers between these countries might explain some of the variance – for example in Japan a much higher proportion of people belong to the non-travellers group than in Norway. However, there are no linear relationships between subjective social status and the share of non-travellers.

This suggests that that people in these countries perceive the social hierarchy somewhat differently. In other words, there are cultural differences that explain how people locate themselves in the social strata compared to others in their society or in their reference group. This study investigates whether the relationship between holidaying and subjective social status holds even after controlling for cultural variation, in other words, whether there is universalist rather than country specific relationship between the two factors. Thus, in the multivariate analysis, country of residence is used as a control variable.

Unfortunately, because the analysis is based on cross-sectional data, no implications can be drawn about causality. The linear relationship found may mean that those not able to make holiday trips locate themselves lower in the social strata. Alternatively it may mean that those locating themselves lower in the strata are for some reason less inclined or less able to travel away from home for a holiday. Since there is a link between holidaying and subjective social status the question arises as to whether holidaying still has an impact on the self-assessment after controlling for various individual and country level factors.

Table 2 shows the results from the linear regression for a series of models, designated I–III. Variables are added to the regression in blocks. Model I includes individual level variables, gender, age, education in years, subjective health, marital status, household composition, and employment relation. Thus we are able to control for many factors that may have an effect on the subjective experience of social status. The factors age, education, subjective health, and employment relation explain statistically significantly the group differences in subjective social status. The impact of age is however very small. The subjective feeling of health has most explanatory power. Those with good, very good or excellent health locate themselves higher on the social strata than those with only fair or poor health. Interestingly marriage also gives a status boost, despite increasing numbers of single people. Perhaps unsurprisingly, those with full-time job also locate themselves higher in the social strata than those with no job or temporary or part-time jobs.

In Model II, time use related variables are added. These are holidaying away from home, which is the most relevant independent variable, together with two variables measuring deprivation in terms of money and time. Although subjective feelings of lack of time explain some of the differences between the social status groups, its explanatory power is seemingly smaller than the variable measuring subjective feeling of lack of money. Money seems to matter most, when we locate ourselves on the social strata – again, this is unsurprising. However, even after controlling for monetary resources, holidaying away from home gains statistical significance in the model. Those who have the ability to afford holidaying away from home on yearly bases locate themselves higher in the social strata than the non-travellers.

The results show that travellers' subjective social status is on average .44 higher than that of non-travellers. This means that when controlling for various socio-economic factors, those able to travel away from home for a holiday locate themselves higher in the social strata. The coefficient is however not very large, and also the explanatory power of the model is not very high (R^2 = .40), which indicates that as well as holidaying there are several other factors that have an impact on the subjective positioning of individuals in the social strata.

Table 2   Impact of dependent variables on people's subjective social status, unstandardised coefficients (Beta)

	Model I	Model II	Model III
Gender			
Male	−.03	−.01	−.01
Female	Ref.	Ref.	Ref.
Age	.01***	.00**	.00***
Education	.10***	.09***	.09***
Subjective health			
Good, very good or excellent	.61***	.49***	.54***
Fair or poor	Ref.	Ref.	Ref.
Marital status			
Married	.33***	.24***	.23***
Single, divorced or widowed	Ref.	Ref.	Ref.
Household composition			
Household with children	−.05	−.02	.00
Household without children	Ref.	Ref.	Ref.
Employment relation			
Employed full-time	.29***	.18***	.14***
Other than full-time employed	Ref.	Ref.	Ref.
Holidaying away from home			
Travellers		.44***	.40***
Non-travellers		Ref.	Ref.
Lack of money			
Major obstacle		−.92***	−.82***
Minor or not an obstacle		Ref.	Ref.
Lack of time			
Major obstacle		.06*	.08*
Minor or not an obstacle		Ref.	Ref.
Australia			.36***
Belgium			.29***
Finland			.32***
France			−.51***
Germany			.31***
Ireland			−.27***
Japan			−.60***
Norway			.68***
Sweden			.43***
Switzerland			Ref.
R2	.32	.40	.47

Significance: * p<0.05, ** p<0.01, *** p<0.001

Source: ISSP 2007

In Model III, after controlling for the country, holidaying is still statistically significant in explaining differences in subjective social status. Also age, education, marital status, and subjective health as well as the lack of financial resources have statistical significance in the model. However, there are also statistically significant differences between the countries in how people locate themselves in the social strata. The results do not differ much from those already seen in the Table 1. Norwegians locate themselves highest and Japanese people lowest even when controlling for various individual level factors.

In this case, country variation can be used as a control for cultural variation. Because the relationship between holidaying and subjective social status is still clear after controlling for the country variation, it can be concluded that perceived social status is, in the ten countries, significantly differentiated by the ability to travel away from home for a holiday. Travelling away from home has indeed become so common that those who do not make a holiday trip assess themselves less worthy in the society. However, as stated before, these data have the limitation that they do not allow for causal links to be drawn. Also, without longitudinal panel data, the dynamics of the relationship between holidaying and self-assessment is relatively uncertain in the sense that there may still be some other factors that explain the variation in the subjective social status and the transitions within the social strata. The two groups in the data used in this study, non-travellers and travellers, may inherently differ from each other in the ways that could not have taken into account in this study. Nevertheless, the results show that there is a direct link between the holidaying away from home and how individuals locate themselves in the social strata. The relationship remains even after controlling for various individual level factors and the country of residences. It also persists after controlling for lack of financial resources, which suggests that holidaying *per se* has an impact on the social positioning of individuals. Hence, whatever the reason for the inability to travel away from home for a holiday, the data show it increases a sense of social exclusion.

Discussion and conclusion

Going on holiday has become increasingly common in the modern affluent world. There has been a major change over the last 50 years and trips that were considered too expensive and out of reach in the past are now within reach for most households. In that sense tourism has become a societal norm. However, there are still households that cannot afford a holiday, and that has implications for their status and well-being. This chapter used large-scale survey data to examine whether holidaying away from home on a yearly basis affects individuals' perceptions of their subjective social status. The results show that even when controlling for income and other individual level factors as well as the country of residence, there is a positive relationship between subjective social status and holidaying away from home. This means that holiday trips away from home make individuals feel more worthy and also more included in society. Of course, there are limitations to the data. With cross-sectional data it is impossible to say anything about the causal relationship between holidaying and social status. Although the results from this study indicate that holidays are linked to raised social status, only with a longitudinal panel data can the mechanism that underlies the social stratification effect of holidaying be understood.

Nevertheless, the results show that those excluded from holidaying see themselves as having reduced social status. This is linked to societal expectations. Holidays are generally seen as a way to leave behind the problems of everyday life for a few days, rest and relax, and spend some quality time with the family (see Minnaert & Schapmans, 2009).

Participation in holidays is seen as allowing people to be part of the society around them and participate in the commonly accepted style of life of that society.

In the EU one week's holiday away from home is generally included in the material deprivation indices (Fusco et al., 2011; see also Halleröd et al., 2006; Nolan & Whelan, 2010), meaning that not having a holiday increases the risk of social exclusion. The results from this study support the idea of a holiday's socially inclusive effect. Even after controlling for a number of salient factors, including country of residence, holidaying away from home has a statistically significant impact on subjective social status. Non-travellers locate themselves lower on the social strata than those who are able (and willing) to travel away from home for a holiday.

Consequently, we can conclude that holidaying is a central issue of inequality. Those able to travel away from home for holiday are better off in society than non-travellers – though it must be emphasised again that this study is unable to examine causality. Nevertheless, results from previous studies show a positive effect of supported holiday opportunities in the form of social holidays (see Smith & Hughes, 1999; Minnaert, 2007; Minnaert & Schapmans, 2009) and further research into individuals' ability to use time according to social norms is required

There is debate about whether social tourism should be promoted as a matter of governmental policy (Minnaert et al., this volume). In part this revolves around the values of different societies, and part around the benefits or utility derived by those participating in social tourism. For example Smith and Hughes (1999) argue that holiday is just a temporary release from low income, poor housing, and the harsh reality of life (see also Nawijn, 2010), though they also acknowledge that the harsh reality of life may only be bearable when there is the prospect of some occasional temporary escape. In contrast, Minnaert and Schapmans (2009) found in their quantitative study that social holidays can have a positive effect on various aspects of holidaymakers' daily lives.

Whether the impacts of holidaying away from home for well-being are significant enough to promote social tourism requires further research. This study focused on the link between holidaying and subjective social status. Based on the results, one way to reduce social inequalities would be to offer individuals and families from low-income groups the possibility of even short holiday trips away from home. Whether governments should promote such policies is a national political decision. However, more detailed research on the benefits generated by social tourism would aid decision-making. That in turn would require more resources for (multinational) data collection – and increased interest from political decision-makers in social tourism.

References

Batty, E. & Flint, J. (2010) *Self-Esteem, Comparative Poverty and Neighbourhoods.* Sheffield: CRESR.

Clarke, J., & Critcher, C. (1985). *The devil makes work: Leisure in capitalist Britain.* Basingstoke: Macmillan.

Commission of the European Communities. (1993). *Towards a Europe of solidarity.* Brussels: CEC.

Dawson, D. (1988). Leisure and the definition of poverty. *Leisure Studies, 7*(3), 221–231.

Evans, M. D. R., & Kelley, J. (2004). Subjective social location: Data from 21 nations. *International Journal of Public Opinion Research, 16*(1), 3–38.

Fusco, A., Guio A. & Marlier, E. (2011). Income poverty and material deprivation in European countries. *CEPS/INSTEAD Working Paper Series 2011-04.* Luxembourg: CEPS/INSTEAD

Gilbert, D., & Abdullah, J. (2002). A study of the impact of the expectation of a holiday on an individual's sense of well-being. *Journal of Vacation Marketing, 8*(4), 352–361.

Halleröd, B., Larsson, D., Gordon, D., & Ritakallio, V. (2006). Relative deprivation: A comparative analysis of Britain, Finland and Sweden. *Journal of European Social Policy, 16*(4), 328–345.

Haukeland, J. V. (1990). Non-travelers: The flip side of motivation. *Annals of Tourism Research, 17*(2), 172,en>184.

Haulot, A. (1981). Social tourism: Current dimensions and future developments. *International Journal of Tourism Management, 2*(3), 207–212.

Hughes, H. L. (1991). Holidays and the economically disadvantaged. *Tourism Management, 12*(3), 193–196.

Lindemann, K. (2007). The impact of objective characteristics on subjective social position. *Trames, 11*(61/56), 54–68.

Mergoupis, T., & Steuer, M. (2003). Holiday taking and income. *Applied Economics, 35*(3), 269–284.

Minnaert, L. (2007). *Social tourism: A potential policy to reduce social exclusion?* Paper presented at the 39th annual UTSG conference, 3–5 January 2007, Harrogate.

Minnaert, L., & Schapmans, M. (2009). Tourism as a form of social intervention: The holiday participation centre in Flanders. *Journal of Social Intervention: Theory and Practice, 18*(3), 42–61.

Minnaert, L., Maitland, R., & Miller, G. (2006). Social tourism and its ethical foundations. *Tourism, Culture & Communication, 7*(1), 7–17.

Nawijn, J. (2010). The holiday happiness curve: A preliminary investigation into mood during a holiday abroad. *International Journal of Tourism Research, 12*(3), 281–290.

Nawijn, J., Marchand, M. A., Veenhoven, R., & Vingerhoets, A. J. (2010). Vacationers happier, but most not happier after a holiday. *Applied Research in Quality of Life, 5*(1), 35–47.

Nolan, B., & Whelan, C. T. (2010). Using non-monetary deprivation indicators to analyse poverty and social exclusion in rich counties: Lessons from Europe? *Journal of Policy Analysis and Management, 29*(2), 305–323.

Quinn, B., & Stacey, J. (2010). The benefits of holidaying for children experiencing social exclusion: Recent Irish evidence. *Leisure Studies, 29*(1), 29–52.

Richards, G. (1998). Time for a holiday? *Time & Society, 7*(1), 145–160.

Rodgers, G. (1995). What is special about a social exclusion approach? In G. Rodgers, C. Gore, & J. B. Figueiredo (Eds), *Social exclusion: Rhetoric, reality, responses* (pp. 43–56). Geneva: International Labour Organization.

Sen, G. (1999) Engendering Poverty Alleviation: Challenges and Opportunities. *Development and Change, 30* (3), 685–692.

Sirgy, M., Phillips, R. & Rahtz, D. (2011) *Community Quality – of – Life Indicators: Best Cases V.* Dordrecht: Springer Publishers

Smith, V., & Hughes, H. (1999). Disadvantaged families and the meaning of the holiday. *International Journal of Tourism Research, 1*(2), 123–133.

Urry, J. (1990). *The tourist gaze: Leisure and travel in contemporary societies.* London: Sage

Accessible social tourism as a social policy strategy for healthy ageing: the relationship between tourism and functional health in older adults

S. Carretero, M. Ferri, and J. Garcés

Polibienestar Research Institute. University of Valencia (Spain).

The number of dependent elderly people is increasing in the European Union, which can be linked to demographic and epidemiological changes. This represents a challenge for the sustainability of the European governments and families, who must react to the increasing need of long-term care. In response to this situation, national and international organisations have started to take measures to prevent dependency situations and improve the health, independent living and quality of life of older adults. In this context, tourism, as a widely available service and resource and due to its relationship with health benefits, could be used as a strategy to promote healthy and active ageing and limit the number of dependent older people in the future.

This chapter is an initial enquiry into its field that analyses the relationship between travel activity and functional health in older adults. Thirty older adults who travelled and thirteen who did not travel during the previous year (n = 43) were randomly selected from six centres that organise leisure activities for elderly people in the city of Valencia and surroundings (Spain) during the year 2011. The two groups were compared in the following variables, collected through a questionnaire composed by both self-designed and standardised instruments: (i) participation in tourism during the previous year, (ii) functional health (self-perceived health, functional capacity, and social integration), (iii) the use of social and health services and (iv) socio-demographic data.

The research showed positive relationships between tourism and elderly people's self-perceived health and functional capacity for carrying out the instrumental activities of daily life. These findings provide initial evidence that tourism has the potential to promote healthy and active ageing and highlight the need for further research in this field.

Introduction

The number of dependent older people is increasing and projections show that this trend is likely to continue. This represents a challenge for governments and families who must respond to the increasing long-term care (LTC) needs of a growing dependent population (Garcés et al., 2002; Carretero et al., 2007). In fact, the EU-27 LTC expenditure is expected to increase from 1.20 per cent in 2007 to 2.50 per cent of the Gross Domestic Product (GDP) in 2060 (European Commission, 2009). Families, besides the burden of care for their loved ones (Carretero et al., 2007), are assuming between 50 to 90 per cent of the overall costs of LTC (Triantafillou et al., 2010), representing between the 20.10 per cent and 36.80 per cent of the European GDP (Gianelli et al., 2010).

In this framework, the European Strategy 2020 and the Member States have declared their interest to promote measures focused on improving the sustainability and efficiency of social and health systems in LTC provision and developing strategies of healthy and active ageing in order to allow elderly people to live longer independently. Active ageing is defined by the World Health Organisation (WHO) as the process of optimising opportunities to enhance quality of life as people age. It allows people to realise their potential for physical, social and mental well-being throughout the life course and to participate in society according to their needs, desires and capacities, while providing them with adequate protection, security and care (WHO, 2004). From this definition, it can be said that not only physical exercise is important to guarantee elderly people's well-being, but also social and mental activities should be promoted.

In this sense, some studies have linked tourism participation with relevant positive effects on the health of some socially excluded groups, understanding health as a state of complete physical, mental and social well-being (WHO, 1946). Gilbert and Abdullah (2003) linked holidaying with higher level of subjective well-being, in terms that people that enjoy travelling feel much satisfied with life and indicated more positive effects. Quinn et al. (2008) have detected a positive effect on the well-being of children belonging to poor resources families that participate in programmes of social tourism, in terms of increase their possibilities of socialising and self-esteem, among others. McCabe et al. (2010) also linked better self-reported measures of well-being with tourism participation of low income families. Other scholars have also found positive relationships between indicators of functional capacity and tourism among groups of disabled people, with improvements in physical efficiency, capacity (Bergier et al., 2010) and feelings of self-sufficiency, independency and safety (Stilling & Nicolaisen, 2010). Similarly, older people that participate in social tourism programmes felt healthier (PriceWaterHouseCoopers, 2004) and perceived positive effects in their physical and mental health after travelling (Paulo et al., 2004). Moreover, McCabe (2009) highlighted demonstrable impacts of holidaying in improvements in mental health, particularly related to the stress and the stress related with illness. Other studies have associated tourism participation with the social integration of their tourists (Quinn et al., 2008; McCabe, 2009), an increase of personal and family relationships in low income families (Quinn et al., 2008; Minnaert et al., 2009) and in people with disabilities (Bergier et al., 2010)

These observed benefits of tourism on health and well-being, together with the fact that tourism is a widely available service that involves physical and social activities, lead to the proposition that tourism could be used as a strategy of active and healthy ageing. Thus, tourism could contribute to stop the increase of dependent older people and, consequently, to the sustainability of social and health systems. In this framework, Accessible Social Tourism, social tourism focused on elderly and disabled people, has recently received the interest of national and European organisations in order to promote tourism for older adults, mainly motivated by the need to adapt society to the demographic changes and to an economic downturn affecting the tourism sector. For example, the European Commission (EC) launched the *Calypso* programme in 2009, aiming to increase the quality of life of European disadvantaged citizens, among them pensioners and over-65s who cannot afford or are daunted by the challenges of organizing a holiday (EC, 2010). At national level it highlights Spain which is the country with longer experience in promoting social tourism programmes for elderly people through the Institute of Elderly and Social Services (IMSERSO). Also, there are other countries with similar initiatives, like France which has developed programmes to promote holidaying in the country for people over 60 years old in the low season. Despite this fairly recent focus on Accessible Social Tourism, a study made after a year of the launch of the *Calypso* programme (EC, 2010) revealed that in most European countries only a segment of the senior population has the financial means to enable travel for holidaying.

To carry out research on the benefits of tourism participation could therefore be part of a strategy to convince private and public tourism entities to promote Accessible Social Tourism. In this sense, this study investigates whether the benefits of social tourism reported on the health of some socially excluded groups, detected in previous studies, can also be applied to older people. Particularly, the research focuses on studying the relationship between tourism participation and the functional health of elderly people, and its relationship with the consumption of health and social care services. This is the first time that this topic has been examined – this is an under-researched area in tourism studies (Minnaert et al., 2009) – and it would help to propose first recommendations to improve the studies in this field and to promote tourism among the elderly.

Methodology

Sample

In this pilot study, a sample of 65+ years old people were randomly selected from six centres that organise leisure activities for elderly in the city of Valencia and surroundings (Spain). The criteria for selection were: to be 65 years old or over, to voluntarily agree to participate in the study and to allow us to use the data collected in an aggregated and anonymous manner exclusively for this research.

The sample was finally formed by 43 older people between 65 and 91 years old. As the research was focused on evaluating the relationship between tourism and elderly people's functional health, a variable that divided the sample in elderly people who had travelled and elderly people who had not travelled during the last year (2010) was used. From that variable, the sample was divided in two independent groups: 30 older people that travelled (69.8 per cent of the sample) and 13 older people who did not travel (30.2 per cent of the sample) in 2010. Both groups were comparable in the main socio-demographic data characteristics, although there were statistically more men in the sample that travelled ($p > 0.05$; 56.7 per cent of men travelled compared to only 23.1 per cent of women). In Table 1 below, the socio-demographic characteristics of the sample and the two groups of comparison are showed.

Procedure for data compilation

The data collection was based on a questionnaire composed by self-designed and standardised instruments (see below). Six leisure centres for older adults of the city of Valencia and its surroundings (Spain) agreed to participate in the study. Firstly, we contacted the leisure centres via the telephone and explained to them the objectives of the research, the content of the study and the anonymity of data, and finally asked them for their collaboration. Once we had their agreement, we went to the leisure centres in order to contact older people who wanted to answer the questionnaire. The questionnaires were self-completed by the elderly people, developing in some cases into personal interviews when the participants had problems with reading and understanding the questions.

Table 1 Socio-demographic data of the sample and by groups (elderly people who travelled and elderly people who did not travel): %, $\overline{X}$ and significance test (t and x^2)

n = 43

		Sample (n=43)		Elderly people who travelled (n=30)		Elderly people who did not travel (n=13)		Differences (travelled/ not travelled)	
								x2 / t	p
Gender	Male	20	46.5%	17	56.7%	3	23.1%	x2= 4.113	0.04*
	Female	23	53.5%	13	43.3%	10	77.0%		
Age	Average	75.3		74.1		78.2		t= 1.861	0.07 -
Marital Status	Single	2	4.7%	1	3.3%	1	7.7%	x2= 5.185	0.27
	Divorced	3	7.0%	2	6.7%	1	7.7%		
	Married	22	51.1%	18	60.0%	4	30.8%		
	Widow / widower	14	32.6%	8	26.7%	6	46.2%		
	Separated	1	2.3%	0	0.0%	1	7.7%		
	NRa	1	2.3%	1	3.3%	0	0.0%		
Highest grade of education completed	Incomplete primary	25	58.1%	18	60.0%	7	53.9%	x2=6.887	0.33
	High school graduate	7	16.3%	3	10.0%	4	30.8%		
	Vocational training of 1 course	1	2.3%	1	3.3%	0	0.0%		
	Vocational training of 2 courses	1	2.3%	1	3.3%	0	0.0%		
	Bachelor degree	3	7.0%	3	10.0%	0	0.0%		
	Three years degree	1	2.3%	0	0.0%	1	7.7%		
	Five years degree	4	9.3%	3	10.0%	1	7.7%		
	NR	1	2.3%	1	3.3%	0	0.0%		
Income source	Wage	1	2.3%	1	3.3%	0	0.0%	x2=2.544	0.64
	Unemployment benefit	1	2.3%	1	3.3%	0	0.0%		
	Retirement pension	37	86.1%	24	80.0%	13	100.0%		
	Invalidity pension	2	4.7%	2	6.7%	0	0.0%		
	Widow's /widower's pension	1	2.3%	1	3.3%	0	0.0%		
	NR	1	2.3%	1	3.3%	0	0.0%		
Wage level	Less than 532,51€	4	9.3%	2	6.7%	2	15.4%	x2=2.838	0.73
	Between 532,51€ and 1.062,02€	23	53.5%	16	53.3%	7	53.9%		
	Between 1.062,02€ and 1.597,53€	8	18.6%	6	20.0%	2	15.4%		
	Between 1.597,53€ and 2.130,04€	2	4.7%	2	6.7%	0	0.0%		
	More than 2.130,04€	1	2.3%	1	3.3%	0	0.0%		
	NR	5	11.6%	3	10.0%	2	15.4%		
People living in the same house	Alone	10	23.3%	7	23.3%	3	23.1%	t=0.292	0.77
	With one person	25	58.1%	17	56.7%	8	61.5%		
	With 2 persons	6	14.0%	4	13.3%	2	15.4%		
	With 4 persons	1	2.3%	1	3.3%	0	0.0%		
	NR	1	2.3%	1	3.3%	0	0.0%		
	Average	1.0		1.0		0.2			
Living arrangements	I live in …								
	… my house alone	10	23.3%	7	23.3%	3	23.1%	x2= 11,768	0.11
	… my house with my partner	18	41.7%	14	46.7%	4	30.8%		
	… my house with my children	4	9.3%	1	3.3%	3	23.1%		
	… my house with my partner and my children	4	9.3%	4	13.3%	0	0.0%		
	… my house with a relative	2	4.7%	1	3.3%	1	7.7%		
	… my house with a person who is not from my family	1	2.3%	0	0.0%	1	7.7%		
	… my house with persons from a University Programme	1	2.3%	0	0.0%	1	7.7%		
	… in the house of a relative	2	4.7%	2	6.7%	0	0.0%		
	NR	1	2.3%	1	3.3%	0	0.0%		

Note: The significant differences at 0.05 are marked with *

a NR= No Response

Following ethical principles in research, older adults were asked to provide their informed consent to participate in the study. The informed consent was collected through a cover sheet to be carefully read, approved and signed by the individuals before continuing with the questionnaire. The informed consent gave specific information on the research entity – the Polibienestar Research Institute of the University of Valencia – the research aims and legal aspects in relation with the study such as anonymity of data, right to withdraw at any time from the research, etc. The respondents were then asked to sign the informed consent page. In order to respect the anonymity of the responses, this signed page was separated from the questionnaire. Moreover, the questionnaire was designed using uncomplicated language and a suitable letter size and document structure according to specific needs of elderly people in research.

Variables and instruments

In order to test the objective to assess the relationship between tourism and the functional health of older adults, the following variables were evaluated:

a.   Participation in tourism during last year
b.   Functional health (self-perceived health, functional capacity and social integration)
c.   Use of social and health services
d.   Demographic data.

Standardised and self-designed instruments were combined in a unique full evaluation questionnaire in order to measure these variables.

The *participation in tourism during last year* measured if the surveyed elderly people had travelled or not during the previous year (2010). This variable allowed us to divide the sample in two groups: elderly who travelled in 2010 (travellers) and elderly who did not travel during the previous year (non-travellers).

The *functional health of the elderly people* was measured through their self-perceived health, functional capacity and social integration.

- *Self-perceived health* was evaluated with the Spanish version of SF-36 (Alonso et al., 1995). This instrument provides a profile of the health status of a surveyed person and is one of the most used instruments in Spain for descriptive studies for measuring quality of life related to health and evaluating therapeutic interventions (Vilagut et al., 2005). It is composed of thirty-six items that form eight dimensions of health that can be combined in two resumed values: physical health and mental health. The eight dimensions of SF-36 are the following (Ware, 2012):
  - Physical functioning: level to which the individual's health limits physical activities such as bathing, dressing or vigorous activities.
  - Role-physical: level to which individual's physical health restrict his or her participation in work or other daily activities.
  - Bodily pain: intensity of the pain suffered by the individual and limitations caused by this pain.
  - General health: individual self-evaluation of personal health.
  - Vitality: feelings of energy and tiredness.
  - Social functioning: level to which emotional and physical problems interfere in individual's normal social activities.

- • Role-emotional: level to which emotional problems interfere in individual's work or daily activities.
- • Mental functioning: feelings of nervousness, depression, peaceful, happiness and calm.

The answer options are likert scales scored from zero (worst health state) to one hundred (better health state). For evaluating the scores achieved by the groups of the sample, we compared them with a Spanish reference population value (Alonso et al., 1998). Although shortened versions of SF-36 are available, the extended version was used here because it allows a deeper evaluation of the different dimensions of health mentioned.

- *Functional capacity* was measured through the capacity of the elderly people to carry out independent activities of daily life (IADL) and their cognitive status.
  - The capacity of the person to carry out IADL was evaluated with the Lawton & Brody Index (Lawton and Brody, 1969). The index involves the evaluation of the life functions necessary for maintaining a person's immediate environment. The index evaluates the capacity to carry out eight activities which are: cleaning, doing the laundry, cooking, shopping, using the phone, using transport, managing one's medication and managing money. These activities are mainly related to housework as such the whole index was used for women (eight daily activities) and the reduced version for men (five daily activities), due to the social differences that are apparent in housework duties in people of this age group. This index gives to each item (activity) a value of zero (some grade of dependency) or one (independent) depending on the answer given by the person. The final score goes from zero (maximum dependent) to eight for woman or five for men (total independent). This index is one of the most used instruments at international level and the most used in geriatrics centres in Spain to evaluate the capacity to carry out IADL because of its reliability (Lyons et al., 2002).
  - *Cognitive status* was measured with the Short Portable Mental Status Questionnaire – SPMSQ (Pfeiffer, 1975). It evaluates the cognitive decline through the mistakes that the surveyed person makes in ten items. Depending on the number of mistakes made by the individual the test gives a grade of cognitive decline that goes from normal cognitive decline (for people who make between zero and two mistakes) to severe cognitive decline (if the person makes between eight and ten mistakes). For scoring the SPMSQ, certain rules are followed to consider an answer correct or incorrect. For example, the date of birth was considered correct if the surveyed person has answered the same date in this part of the questionnaire and in the socio-demographic data part.
- *Social integration* was measured with the Berkman-Syme Social Network Index (Berkman & Syme, 1979). This instrument assesses four types of social connections: marital status, sociability, church group membership and membership of other community organisations. It measures the grade of social integration and support, scoring the individual from most isolated (zero) to most integrated (four). Although it is not designed for elderly people, we have used this instrument for two main reasons: first, it considers more kinds of relationships than the instruments exclusively designed for older people, and second, other indexes that measure social relationships among elderly people are mainly designed for the context of care homes and not for the home environment.

- The *use of social and health services* is measured through thirteen self-designed items which collect information related to the last twelve months' use of health services (number of medical consultations, use frequency of hospitalisation and emergency service, types of health professionals visited, setting of the visits and tests carried out) and social services (use of home help service and caregiver support).
- *Socio-demographic data* on gender, age, marital status, education level, income source, wage level, household size, relationship with people that live in the same house, disability certificate entitlement and recognition of any dependency degree were also collected.

Statistical analysis

In order to meet the objectives of the research, statistical analysis were carried out using the SPSS Statistics Version 19. Descriptive analyses were run in order to know the demographic characteristics of the sample. Bivariate comparative tests were also carried out between the two groups (elderly people who travelled and elderly people who did not travel in 2010) to detect significant differences on their functional health and their use of health and social services. t-Student and Chi-Squared tests for continuous and categorical variables were respectively used at 0.05 significance level.

Results

Results of the relationship between tourism and the functional health of older adults

To assess the relationship between tourism participation and the functional health of elderly people, both groups (older adults who travelled and elderly people who did not travel in the last year) were compared in the variables of self-perceived health, capacity to carry out IADL, cognitive decline and social integration.

Regarding *self-perceived health* of the elderly people, some health dimensions were measured using the SF-36 instrument that scores from 0 to 100 eight different health dimensions. Results showed (Table 2) that older adults who travelled during last year had an average of physical health of 76.5 (S.D. =16.4) and mental health of 78.8 (S.D. =15.8); while elderly people who did not travel during last year had an average of physical health of 67.0 (S.D. =21.7) and mental health of 74.7 (S.D. =12.3). These results revealed that elderly people who travelled last year reached higher values of both dimensions (physical and mental health) than elderly people who did not travel in 2010. Likewise, elderly people who travelled presented health values closer to the population value reference than elderly people who did not travel. However, all these differences were not statistically significant (p>0.05).

When we looked at the eight health dimensions of the SF-36, results reflected that elderly people who travelled in 2010 presented higher levels of health than non-travellers in seven of the eight dimensions. These differences were statistically significant (p<0.05) in physical functioning and vitality. Thus, elderly people who travelled had greater physical functioning ($\overline{X}$ =81.0; S.D. = 17.3) which is a dimension of physical health and means that they had more physical capacity to participate in vigorous and moderate activities, such as carrying the shopping bag, climbing one or several floors, bending and kneeling, walking one or several blocks and bathing or dressing themselves, than elderly people who did not travel ($\overline{X}$ =62.8; S.D. =27.3). Also, elderly people who travelled had higher vitality ($\overline{X}$ =68.0; S.D. =18.0), which is a dimension of mental health and measures the vitality and energy feelings against the tiredness and feelings of exhaustion, than elderly people who did not travel ($\overline{X}$ =54.2; S.D. =18.8). Moreover, elderly people who did not travel represented a slower physical function and vitality than the general population (p<0.05) and elderly people who travelled had a similar health of the general population in all SF-36 health dimensions (p>0.05).

There were two dimensions in which elderly people who did not travel reached higher levels of health than elderly travellers which were the role-emotional (extent to which the emotional problems interfere in the individual work or daily activities) and health development (assessment of current health compared to last year). But the differences in these dimensions were not statistically significant (p>0.05).

Table 2 $\overline{X}$, S.D. of SF-36 health dimensions and t between elderly people who travelled, elderly people who did not travel (n=43)

		$\overline{X}$	S.D.	T	p	t (population value)	p (population value)
Physical health	Travel	76.5	16.4	1.590	0.12	−0.754	0.46
	Not travel	67.0	21.7			−1.964	0.07
Mental health	Travel	78.8	15.9	0.797	0.43	−0.321	0.75
	Not travel	74.7	12.3			−1.404	0.19
Physical functioning	Travel	81.0	17.3	2.639	0.01*	−1.169	0.25
	Not travel	62.9	27.3			−2.880	0.01*
Role-Physical	Travel	83.9	29.8	0.249	0.81	0.126	0.90
	Not travel	81.3	33.9			−0.199	0.85
Role- emotional	Travel	87.8	30.9	−0.692	0.50	−0.146	0.86
	Not travel	94.4	19.3			1.052	0.32
Vitality	Travel	67.9	18.0	2.199	0.03*	0.308	0.76
	Not travel	54.2	18.8			−2.345	0.04*
Mental functioning	Travel	71.6	22.0	0.891	0.38	−0.403	0.69
	Not travel	65.0	22.2			−1.309	0.22
Social functioning	Travel	85.8	16.7	0.072	0.94	−1.403	0.17
	Not travel	85.4	17.5			−0.925	0.38
Bodily pain	Travel	75.0	21.2	0.590	0.56	−1.032	0.31
	Not travel	70.0	32.4			−0.962	0.36
General health	Travel	66.3	17.2	1.427	0.16	−0.653	0.52
	Not travel	57.7	12.0			−1.916	0.08

Note: The significant differences at 0.05 are marked with *

Secondly, the elderly people's *functional capacity*, referring to the capacity to carry out IADL and cognitive decline, was analysed and compared between both groups (older adults who travelled and elderly who did not travel in the last year). On the one hand, the Lawton and Brody index (1969) that scores from zero (dependent) to eight for women and to five for men (independent) was used to evaluate the elderly's capacity to carry out IADL. Results (Table 3) showed that women and men who travelled last year had slightly higher values (women: $\overline{X}$ = 7.8; S.D. =0.6; men $\overline{X}$ = 4.7; S.D. = 0.5) than women and men who did not travel in 2010 (women $\overline{X}$ = 7.0; S.D. = 1.2; men: $\overline{X}$ = 4.5; S.D. = 4.5). Nevertheless, the analysis revealed that older women who travelled had a better capacity to carry out IADL than older women who did not travel in 2010 (p<0.05). For men, no significant differences were observed.

Table 3 $\overline{X}$, S.D. and t-Student of the Lawton and Brody index (1969) between travellers and non-travellers elderly women and men (n=34).

		$\overline{X}$	S.D.	t	p
Women	Travel	7.8	0.6	2.095	0.05*
	Not travel	7.0	1.2		
Men	Travel	4.7	0.5	0.425	0.68
	Not travel	4.5	0.7		

Note: The significant differences at 0.05 are marked with *

The elderly people's cognitive decline was measured through Pfeiffer SPMSQ (1975). This test did not reveal any difference between elderly people who travelled and who did not travel during the previous year. Both groups made an average of one mistake that means no existence of cognitive decline (Table 4). In the same way, in the classification that provides the Pfeiffer SPMSQ (1975), between normal cognitive and severely impaired, it revealed that (Table 5) 93.3 per cent of elderly travellers were in the normal cognitive state and 92.3 per cent of elderly non-travellers were in this state, with no significant difference between both groups (p>0.05).

Table 4 $\overline{X}$, S.D. and t of number of errors in Pfeiffer SPMSQ (1975) between elderly who travelled and elderly who did not travel (n=43).

		$\overline{X}$	S.D.	t	p
Number of mistakes	Travel	0.9	1.0	−0.199	0.84
	Not travel	1.0	1.0		

Table 5 Cognitive decline by Pfeiffer SPMSQ (1975) of elderly travellers and elderly non-travellers (n and %) and X^2 between both groups (n=43).

	Travel		Not travel		X^2	p
	n	%	n	%		
Normal cognitive state	28	93.33	12	92.31	0.015	0.90
Mildly impaired	2	6.67	1	7.69		
Moderately impaired	0	0.00	0	0.00		
Severely impaired	0	0.00	0	0.00		

Regarding *social integration*, results did not show significant differences between elderly people who travelled and who did not travel during last year. Nevertheless, in the Berkman-Syme index (1979) that scores the person from most isolated to most integrated, as we can see in Table 6, 90.5 per cent of elderly people who travelled were in the middle groups of integration (47.6 per cent in medium grade and 42.9 per cent in medium-high grade) against only 50.0 per cent of elderly people who did not travel who were situated in these grades (20.0 per cent in medium grade and 30.0 per cent in medium-high grade). Thus, 40 per cent of elderly people who did not travel were situated in the low grade of integration while only 9.5 per cent of older adults who travelled were in this low grade.

Table 6   Berkman-Syme Index (1979) n, % and X^2 of elderly people who travelled and who did not travel (n=31).

	Low		Medium		Medium-high		High		X^2	P
	N	%	n	%	N	%	n	%		
Travel	2	9.5	10	47.6	9	42.7	0	0.0	6.975	0.07
Not travel	4	40.0	2	20.0	3	30.0	1	10.0		

Results of the tourism relationship with the use and consumption of social and health resources among older adults.

The use of social and health resources for elderly people who travelled and elderly people who did not travel during last year was also compared in order to know the possible indirect relationship between tourism and cost reductions for the LTC system.

Regarding the use of *health services*, elderly people who travelled and elderly people who did not travel went to the doctor an average of 8 visits per year (travellers S.D. = 8.4; non-travellers S.D. =10.0). In relation to the kind of the doctor visited, 83.3 per cent of elderly people who travelled consulted the family doctor and 63.3 per cent a specialist; 92.3 per cent of elderly people who did not travel consulted the family doctor and 77.0 per cent a specialist. These differences were not significant (p>0.05) so both groups consulted the same kinds of health professionals last year (2010).

Considering the reasons of their consultations (Table 7), elderly people who did not travel visited health professionals more for diagnosis or health problems (53.9 per cent) and for accidents (15.4 per cent) than elderly people who travelled (20.0 per cent and 10.0 per cent, respectively); and elderly travellers visited health professionals more often for check-ups (63.3 per cent) and prescriptions (80.0 per cent) than elderly people who did not travel (46.2 per cent for each). These differences were statistically significant (p<0.05): this means that older adults who travelled in 2010 visit the doctor less than non-travellers for the diagnosis of health problems.

Table 7   reasons to go to the doctor (n and per cent) and X^2 between elderly people who travelled and elderly people who did not travel (n=43).

Reasons to attend the doctor	Travelled		Not travelled		X^2	P
	N	%	n	%		
Diagnosis or health problems	6	20.0	7	53.9	4.617	0.03*
Accident	3	10.0	2	15.4	0.217	0.64
Revision	19	63.3	6	46.2	1.397	0.24
For prescriptions	23	79.7	6	46.2	3.522	0.06

Note: The significant differences at 0.05 are marked with *

With regards to number of hospitalisations and use of emergency services, elderly people who travelled were hospitalised and used the emergency services more (57.1 per cent) than elderly people who did not travel (42.96 per cent), but these differences were not significant.

In the use of *social services*, results in Table 8 showed that elderly people who did not travel used home help service provided in Spain more often (62.5 per cent) than elderly people who travelled (37.5) (p<0.05). This service provides care and support to older adults in personal, domestic, psychological, social, educational, rehabilitative and/or technical aspects of their daily activities and, consequently, enhancing their own autonomy. So, elderly non-travellers received more help in their daily activities than elderly people who travelled in 2010.

Table 8   Elderly people's use of home help service and X² between elderly people who travelled and who did not travel (n=42).

	Travel		Not travel		X²	P
	N	%	n	%		
Home help service	3	37.5	5	62.5	4.602	0.03*

Note: The significant differences at 0.05 are marked with *

Conclusions and discussion

The main aim of this pilot study has been to study the tourism relationship with the functional health of older adults. The results show a positive relationship between tourism and elderly self-perceived health, and capacity to carry out IADL. In this section, the obtained results are analysed and discussed.

First, this research showed that tourism participation has a positive relationship with older adults' *self-perceived health*. In this sense, the results revealed that elderly people who travelled during the last year had better physical health related with their self-care, their capacity of movement (to walk, to climb floors, to bend and to kneel and to take and carry and transport weight) and develop vigorous and moderate activities (physical function); and a better mental health related with energy and vitality feelings against feelings of tiredness and exhaustion (vitality) than elderly people who did not travel. Moreover, elderly people who travelled showed a similar health profile to the general population while elderly people who did not travel had lower physical function and vitality that the general population. So tourism participation could have a relevant positive relationship with the health of the elderly population. It is important to highlight here however that it is likely that people in better health are more likely to travel – further research is needed to investigate the causality between these factors.

There is a lack of studies that analyse the impacts of tourism on elderly people so we cannot compare the obtained relationship with other data in this area. However, the obtained relationship reaffirms the findings of a study about the IMSERSO programme in Spain. In that research, it is proposed that tourism has positive effects on health and quality of life of the programme's users because they felt healthier after travelling (PriceWaterHouseCoopers, 2004). Also, in another study about a similar programme in Chile ('Holidays for senior citizens in the low season', Paulo et al., 2004) positive medical impacts of holidaying on subjective aspects of well-being and physical and mental health are recorded. Both studies link tourism with older adults' health as in this research but they do not provide specific information about the nature of the impact on health. There are however a number of studies that link the participation in tourism of other social excluded groups with health, for example: subjective well-being (EESC, 2006; Bergier et al., 2010), increase of physical efficiency and capacity (Bergier et al., 2010), and mental health related with illness stress (McCabe, 2009). The reason for these positive effects could be explained because travelling involves several activities that are not part of the daily life of elderly people. Among these are a higher level of physical exercise through visits and walks, attendance at entertainment activities, interaction with the natural environment, engagement with culture and increased social contact.

Regarding the last aspect, social interaction, this research has analysed the tourism relationship with the *social integration* of elderly people. The obtained results did not provide evidence of a positive relationship between tourism and the social integration of the participants. However, only a small proportion of surveyed older adults who travelled (9.5 per cent) were in the lowest grade of social integration on the Berkman-Syme index (1979), compared to 40.0 per cent of elderly people who did not travel. In this sense, the way in which data had been collected could have represented a limitation because the participants belong to leisure centres that promote activities for them and integrate them in society. Nevertheless, other studies have demonstrated, in other population groups, the relationship between tourism and an increase and improvement of personal and family relationships (Quinn et al., 2008; Minnaert et al., 2009; <Bergier et al., 2010) and other studies have linked tourism with the social integration of their users (Quinn et al., 2008; McCabe, 2009).

This study also analyses the relationship between tourism and *functional capacity* in two aspects: the capacity to carry out IADL and cognitive capacity. The results showed a positive relationship between tourism and the capacity of elderly women who travelled for developing independently IADL. This positive relationship could be explained because the participation in tourism makes elderly people feel more capable to carry out their daily life and to exercise their memory thanks to the use of public transport, to be responsible of their medication and finances, to organise the journey or activities, to participate in activities that require some concentration or exercise, etc. Thus, mental activity is necessary to preserve intellectual capacity. A reduction of this capacity has relevant effects on the well-being and the quality of life of elderly people because this lack of autonomy is one of the older adults' greatest fears (Larrión, 1999). In this sense, Accessible Social Tourism can potentially support levels of autonomy because tourism could contribute to preserve mental capacity.

This pilot study provides some positive relationships between participation in tourism and a better self-perceived health and higher functional capacity of elderly people. As a result, it can be proposed that tourism could have an influence on physical, mental and social well-being (Lee & Tedeswall, 2005) of elderly tourists and it could be used as social and health policy due to its associated benefits and their potential contribution to reduce *public spending on social care and healthcare* due to travellers' less use of health and social services. The results showed more specifically that elderly people who travelled used the home help service (social resource) less and visited the doctor less often for diagnosis and illness problems (health service) during 2010. These aspects reflect the better health and autonomy of elderly people who travelled compared with the health of non-travellers. Although current research has not provided scientific evidence of this so far, the consequences of not enjoying holidays have been linked to an increase of social expenditure in health and well-being (Hazel, 2005).

To conclude, this pilot study has suggested a first body of evidence that links tourism participation with the elderly's functional health and therefore on the independence and quality of life of elderly people, contributing to their healthy and active ageing. Holidays are shown to potentially have demonstrable impacts connected with many areas of current government policies on health and well-being (McCabe, 2009). Despite the small number of the sample, the obtained results can serve as an exploratory study to be used as a basis for future research. Thus, this study highlights the need of more research in this field in order to analyse the tourism participation effects on older people's health and to obtain solid evidence of this relationship. In particular, whilst the association between better health and tourism seems clear, more research is required to investigate causality. Moreover, more research about the characteristics of elderly tourists is needed in order to adapt tourism resources and policies to their needs and preferences, and to make the tourism sector more accessible for them.

References

Alonso, J., Prieto, L., & Antón, J.M. (1995). La versión española del SF-36 Health Survey (Cuestionario de Salud SF-36): un instrumento para la medida de los resultados clínicos. *Medicina Clínica, 20*(104): 771–776. Barcelona.

Alonso, J., Regidor, E., Barrio, G., Prieto, L., Rodríguez, C., & de la Fuente, L. (1998). Valores poblacionales de referencia de la versión española del Cuestionario de Salud SF-36. *Medicina Clínica, 11*(111): 410–416. Barcelona.

Bergier, B., Bergier, J, & Kubinska, Z. (2010). Environmental determinants of participation in tourism and recreation of people with varying degrees of disability. *Journal of Toxicology and Environmental Health*, Part A (73), Issue 17–18. DOI: 10.1080/15287394.2010.491042

Berkman, L., & Syme, S. (1979). Social networks, host resistance, and mortality: a nine-year follow-up of Alameda county residents. *Am J Epidemiol*, 109: 186–204.

Carretero, S., Garcés, J., & Ródenas, F. (2007). Evaluation of the home help service and its impact on the informal caregiver's burden of dependent elders. *International Journal of Geriatric Psychiatry, 22*(8): 738–749.

EESC (2006). Opinion of the European Economic and Social Committee on Social tourism in Europe (2006/C 318/12). *Official Journal of the European Union* C 318/67.

European Commission (2009). The 2009 Ageing Report: Economic and budgetary projections for the EY-27 Member States. *European Economy*, 2. Luxemburg. 456p.

European Commission (2010). Calypso study. Final Report.

Garcés, J., Zafra, E., Ródenas, F., & Megía, Mª.J. (2002). Estudio sobre demanda y necesidades de asistencia sociosanitaria en la Comunidad Valenciana. Valencia: Generalitat Valenciana, Consellería de Sanitat, Escuela Valenciana de Estudios para la Salud (EVES).

Giannelli, G., Mangiavacchi, L., & Piccoli. L. (2010). GDP and the value of family caretaking: How much does Europe care? *IZA Discussion Papers 5046*.

Gilbert, D., & Abdullah, J. (2003). Holidaying and the sense of well-being. *Annals of Tourism Research, 1*(31): 103–121. DOI:10.1016.

Hazel, N. (2005). Holidays for children and families in need: An exploration of the research and policy context for social tourism in the UK. *Children & Society*, 19: 225–236.

Larrión, J. L. (1999) Valoración geriátrica integral (III). Evaluación de la capacidad funcional del anciano. *Anales Sis San Navarra, 1*(22): 71–84.

Lawton, M. P., & Brody, E. M. (1969). Assessment of older people: self-maintaining and instrumental activities of daily living. *Gerontologist,* 9: 179–186.

Lee, S. H., & Tideswell, C. (2005). Understanding attitudes towards leisure travel and the constraints faced by senior Koreans. *Journal of Vacations Marketing, 3*(11): 249–263.

Lyons, K. S., Zarit, S. H., Sayer, A. G., & Whitlatch, C. J. (2002). Caregiving as a Dyadic Process: Perspectives from Caregiver and Receiver. *Journal of Gerontology, 57*(3), 195–204.

McCabe, S. (2009). Who needs a holiday? Evaluating social tourism. *Annals of Tourism Research, 36*(4), 667–668, DOI:10.1016.

McCabe, S., Joldersma, T., & Chuixiao, L. (2010). Understanding the benefits of social tourism: Linking participation to wellbeing and quality of life. *International Journal of Tourism Research*, 6(12): 761–773. DOI: 10.1002.

Minnaert, L., Maitland, R., & Miller, G. (2009) Tourism and social policy – the value of social tourism. *Annals of Tourism Research, 36*(2): 316–334.

Paulo, P., Carrasco, M., Cabezas, M., Gac, H., Hoyl, T., Duery, P., Petersen, K., & Dussaillant, K. (2004). Impacto biomédico de los viajes en adultos mayores chilenos. *Rev Méd Chile, 132*: 573–578.

Pfeiffer, E. A. (1975). A short portable mental status questionnaire for the assessment of organic brain deficits in elderly patients. *J Am Geriatr Soc, 22*: 433–441.

PriceWaterHouseCoopers. (2004). Estudio sobre el Programa de Vacaciones para mayores del IMSERSO. 48p.

Quinn, B., Griffin, K., & Stacey, J. (2008). Poverty, social exclusion and holidaying: Towards developing policy in Ireland. *Poverty Agency Policy Research Initiative Working Paper*.

Stilling, B., & Nicolaisen, J. (2010). Disabled travel: Not easy, but doable. *Current Issues in Tourism*, (14) Issue 1. DOI: 10.1080/13683500903370159

Triantafillou, J., Naiditch, M., Repkova, K., Stiehr, K., Carretero, S., Emilsson, T., Di Santo, P., Bednarik, R., Brichtova, L., Ceruzzi, F., Cordero, L., Mastroyiannakis, T., Ferrando, M., Mingot, K., Ritter, K., Vlantoni, D. (2010). Informal care in the long-term care system. European Overview Paper. *Interlinks*.

Vilagut, G., Ferrer, M., Rajmil, L., Rebollo, P., Permanyer-Miralda, G., Quintana, J. M., Santed, R., Valderas, J. M., Ribera, A., Domingo-Salvany, A., & Alonso, J. (2005). El cuestionario de Salud SF-36 español: una década de experiencia y nuevos desarrollos. *Gaceta Sanitaria, 19*(2): 135–150.

Ware, J. E. (2012). SF-36 ® Health Survey Update. [ref. 15 March 2012]. Available on: http://www.sf-36.org/tools/SF36.shtml#VERS2

WHO (1946). Preamble to the Constitution of the World Health Organization. International Health Conference, New York, 19 June–22 July 1946. *Official Records of the World Health Organization*, 2, p. 100.

WHO. (2004). *Active ageing: A policy framework*. Madrid. 60p.

CASE STUDY

The International Organisation of Social Tourism (ISTO) working towards a right to holidays and tourism for all[1]

Charles Étienne Bélanger[a] and Louis Jolin[b]

[a]ISTO, Brussels, Belgium; [b]Département d'études urbaines et touristiques, École des sciences de la gestion, Université du Québec à Montréal, Montréal (Québec), Canada

This case study article discusses the history and development of the International Organisation of Social Tourism (ISTO) and its role in social tourism policy and provision today. It will examine the origins of the concept, how it developed in a historical context and how the organisation has responded to the challenges this has brought. The main milestones of the organisation will be contextualised: from the foundation of ISTO (then Bureau International du Tourisme Social, BITS which became ISTO in September 2010) in 1963, over the Montreal Declaration in 1996 to the Addendum of Aubagne in 2006. Although social tourism is historically mainly a European phenomenon, ISTO is a global organisation, and the article will therefore highlight examples of projects in other parts of the world. In conclusion, the article will review the most recent challenges that face social tourism today and propose avenues for the future as proposed by ISTO.

Introduction

Because holidays are an integral part of life in many of our societies, one may forget that there is still a large section of the population for whom the right to a holiday and tourism is but a distant dream. This is why it is the mission of the International Organisation of Social Tourism (ISTO) to promote access to holidays, leisure and tourism for the greatest number. ISTO supports the development of social tourism because the organisation is a firm believer in the potential positive social impacts of tourism on participants – therefore, it lobbies the actors who can play a role in social tourism provision. ISTO has now been active for 48 years in the establishment of a tourism for all, characterised by sustainability and solidarity, as an intrinsic part of the tourism industry.

ISTO: a key actor in the growth of social tourism

To fully comprehend the importance of ISTO, it may be useful to situate the organisation in the wider context of the development and growth of social tourism. The desire of a growing number of individuals to participate in holidays became apparent after the Second World

War, and this led to the formation of a number of organisations – not-for-profit organisations, unions, cooperatives, youth groups – offering a number of holiday options to the wider population. These organisations started to build national and international networks. On an institutional level, this evolution roots in the 1936 Holiday with Pay Convention, obtained via pressure of workers movements, which was recognised in the 1948 *Universal Declaration of Human Rights* (article 24) and the *International Covenant on Economic, Social and Cultural Rights* (article 7.d). On the basis of these developments, tourism and leisure grew rapidly and in certain countries this led to social tourism policies being established.

These social tourism policies tended to focus on two main areas, often referred to as *support for the infrastructure* (aide au patrimoine) and *support for the person* (aide à la personne). The former related to investment in built facilities (construction, renovation and modernisation), equipment and infrastructures. The latter referred to investing in making holiday participation possible for individuals. These policies resulted in innovative initiatives and policies and allowed millions of persons to exert their right to a holiday. This period is often considered as the start of the democratisation of tourism, and social tourism underwent a particular growth (Bélanger, 1999).

It is in this context that ISTO was created in 1963 by a number of organisations that aimed to provide a permanent platform where social tourism issues could be discussed at an international level. The organisation was then called BITS (Bureau International du Tourisme Social) and addressed issues such as financing holidays, increasing holiday participation rates, youth tourism, tourism and culture, family tourism, tourism and the environment, seasonality, rural tourism and tourism as a catalyst for development and integration. These themes and many other were also discussed in biannual ISTO congresses and were further explored in a range of publications.

ISTO also gained influence with international organisations such as the World Tourism Organisation (UNWTO), and this influence was particularly significant in the preparation of the 1980 *Manila Declaration* on social tourism, signed by 107 states and 91 observers. The Manila Declaration synthesised the fundamental ideas about the nature and the beneficiaries of social tourism, and these ideas are still widely adopted in the international community. Not only does the declaration emphasis a person's right to a holiday, it also expresses the notion – also present in the UNWTO statutes – that tourism can play an important role in furthering the economic and social growth of developing countries (Bélanger, 1999). Today, issues relating to the right to holidays are also part of the Global Tourism Code of Ethics, adopted by the UNWTO in 1999. Article 7 of this Code specifically mentions social tourism.

ISTO has thus been a driving factor in the development of social tourism and has steered the big international debates around the subject. The organisation has also played a key role in updating the definition and conceptualisation of social tourism, which has evolved strongly over the years.

Social tourism: concept and evolution

In the official statutes of ISTO, social tourism has been defined as the effects and phenomena that result from the participation in tourism and more specifically from the participation of low-income groups. This participation is made possible or is facilitated by initiatives of a well-defined social nature (Statutes, BITS, 2003). This definition being rather general, ISTO soon realised the need for a first reference text to define its actions, and those of organisations active in social tourism provision, better.

It was with this aim that in 1972, at the General Assembly in Vienna, ISTO adopted the Charter of Vienna. This charter represents social tourism as a "fundamental social fact of our times" and lists a number of action principles that enable tourism to encourage a process of personal growth and enrichment, which can be seen as a confirmation of the liberty of the individual. The text also highlights the need to continue permanent efforts to educate the public and provide information to those who are interested in social tourism, so that tourism can carry out its due humanistic vocation. Finally, it is emphasised that no social policy should be without a social tourism policy, and this should stay at the forefront of the attention of all governments (Vienna Charter, BITS, 1972).

The Charter reflects a time when several social tourism promoters gave the sector a socio-educational, even a socio-political, aspect. The organised activities on holiday were often inspired by the ideals of the popular educational movements and had a strong militant character (Jolin, 2003).

In the 1980s, a number of global changes took place that deeply affected the social tourism sector (Froidure, 1997). This period was characterised by the domination of a liberal ideology with emphasis on free competition, with a reduced role of the state. The economic crisis resulted in forced hypercompetitiveness. Many states reduced their budgets because of new attitudes towards social policy, which caused the inequalities in society to increase because of growing unemployment levels, social exclusion and integration problems for immigrants.

The direct impacts of this on the social tourism sector soon became apparent:

- an almost complete halt to public investment because of budget cuts;
- the need for associations to transform into veritable social enterprises;
- the need for associations to develop new, profitable client bases.

These changes forced the social tourism sector to reposition itself and led to ISTO updating the social tourism concept. The new concept took into account a new worldwide context characterised by the collapse of socialist economies and the emergence of a new 'tourism for all' in certain countries of Latin America, Africa and Asia.

The result of this process in 1996 was a second reference document, the *Montreal Declaration* (BITS, 1996). The document proposes a humanistic and social vision of tourism and mainly differs from the Vienna Charter by placing greater emphasis on responsible management strategies: by advocating long-term and sustainable strategies for an expert form of tourism that respects the environment and the people in it; and by redefining the characteristics of social tourism, starting that 'it is not the legal statutes or the procedures that are used that make sure businesses classify as social tourism, but it is the actions they take towards a clearly defined and pursued goal' (Montreal Declaration, 1996).

As well as emphasising the importance of holiday participation, the *Montreal Declaration* also introduces a sense of solidarity between the tourist and the host population, confirming that social tourism is opposite to invasive mass tourism that overburdens local resources (Jolin, 2003).

Ten years later, in 2006, a new text was adopted to reinforce this new direction. At the ISTO conference in Aubagne en Provence, the *Addendum to the Montreal Declaration, towards a tourism of development and solidarity* was signed: this addendum emphasises the role of tourism as a development tool and places a much greater importance on host populations.

Today's objectives and challenges

It is on the basis of these reference texts that the current objectives and challenges for social tourism and ISTO are summarised here. They can be defined on three levels: tourism for all, solidarity tourism and the lack of resources (Mignon, 2002).

Tourism for all

Tourism for all refers to the goal to include as many persons as possible into tourism and leisure. Even today, in a country like France, for example, which is one of the most visited worldwide tourism destinations and which has a well-developed social tourism policy, almost 40% of the population does not take a holiday. This proportion is likely to be much higher than in less developed countries.

Tourism for all is thus a continued priority for ISTO and the social tourism sector: for national governments and states, for the social organisations and for the tourism operators. In several countries, there is currently a lack of social policies regarding tourism, and this is a problem that the social tourism actors by themselves cannot always overcome. It is the role of the public sector to encourage and support holiday participation in the different layers of society and to develop strategies that are tailored to different target groups.

The main current target markets for a social tourism policy are young people, families, senior citizens and persons with a disability. These existing social tourism policies have often been shown to have substantial economic benefits. The youth tourism market has received particular attention in a growing number of countries: specific strategies have been developed to better inform this target group of the different options that are available for travel or to develop destinations as particularly attractive for the youth market. This was also the theme of a colloquium organised by ISTO Americas in 2007 in Mexico City.

Similarly for the family market, there has been an interest in product development in terms of accommodation, activities and entertainment that is suited to different types of families and that is often combined with measures to encourage and support holiday participation. These allow millions of persons to exert their 'right to a holiday'. Other products are particularly developed for certain groups in society. This is, for example, the case with immigrant groups for whom the idea of a holiday may take a different meaning as their integration evolves and who may have specific needs that need to be considered[2].

The integration of Tourism for All in tourism policies and the development of greater cooperation between public and private sectors are important priorities for ISTO. In this context, it may be surprising that many important tourism destinations like France, Spain and Mexico have a social tourism policy at national and/or regional levels. This shows that social tourism is no threat but a catalyst for domestic tourism and compatible with a focus on developing international tourism. It is a telling fact that in many, particularly developing, countries, social tourism and access to holidays is only developed in times of crisis, when the influx of foreign tourists diminishes because of conflicts or periodical natural disasters.

Solidarity tourism

Solidarity tourism aims to introduce the tourist to concrete forms of solidarity with the host community. This solidarity can take different forms: the tourists may support a local development project or contribute to a fundraising initiative (French National Union of Tourism and Outdoor Leisure Associations [UNAT], 2002). This is a new challenge for ISTO and an area where the organisation would like to assume a certain degree of leadership. One could ask though why an organisation which is dedicated to tourism for the greatest number would be interested in tourism forms that generally take place in small groups and that are often inaccessible to many because of price?

The first argument is the fact that social tourism, as defined in the *Montreal Declaration*, is based on the intrinsic values that underlie sustainable tourism, and those are also at the basis of solidarity tourism. Sustainable tourism has three main principles: 'a tourism that can be supported in the long term on an ecological level that furthers equality on an ethical level, and is viable on an economic level' (Caire & Rouillet-Caire, 2003).

The second motivation is the principle that access to tourism sites and resources, and a share in the benefits of tourism should not only be a reality for tourists and visitors but also for the host community. It has been repeatedly demonstrated that tourism income is not always distributed widely and equitably in the host community, which is illustrated by the living conditions of some populations who are near tourist sites.

Finally, the tools that have been developed for social tourism can be used in a special-ised tourism form that integrates the principles of solidarity tourism. The associations and the cooperative sector can play a role in the promotion and commercialisation of a suchlike offer for their members.

At present, most associations that are the members of ISTO already engage with host communities and practice solidarity. Still, ISTO is aware that in recent years a great number of associations and NGOs have developed outside its network and that the internet has provided tourism associations and cooperation NGOs with a platform for discussion.

The active participation of ISTO in the first three editions of the International Forum of Solidarity Tourism (FITS), that took place, respectively, in Marseille (2003), Tuxtla Gutiérrez au Chiapas (2006) and Bamako (2008), and the development of national networks such as ATES (Association for Equitable and Solidarity Tourism) in France and AITR (Italian Association for Responsible Tourism) in Italy, in which a number of ISTO members are very active, are indicative of these efforts.

There are numerous challenges that affect the development of solidarity tourism. The main ones are the definition of selection criteria, the development of networks, the com-munication of good practices the commercialisation of initiatives and the diversification of the client base. Overcoming these challenges may lead to a change from the development of tourism towards a tourism of development (Tonini, 2003).

A lack of resources

The third area where ISTO is active is by no means the least challenging: the accessibility and the solidarity goals of the organisation require a constant mobilisation of human and financial resources. Even if associations, cooperatives and NGOs sometimes have access to their own resources to achieve these objectives, either because of their entrepreneurial spirit or because of their volunteers, this may not be seen as a reason for public bodies to stop taking up their social responsibility in this area.

The need for networks and effective management strategies is also felt in the sector of social and solidarity tourism, just as in other tourism sectors.

There is a need for the associations and other organisations, most of which are active at a local or national level, to integrate into an international network. They should 'engage in the challenging project to reform or form a dynamic partnership structure with international organisations, public powers (national, regional and local governments), and social part-ners, not in the least the unions and the representatives of the social economy in the voluntary sector: for example cooperative movements, community development corporations and many more...' (Mignon, 2002).

Finally, one of the important conditions to address the lack of resources is the need to situate social tourism actions at the heart of the tourism industry by bringing ideas and proposing co-operations with the commercial tourism sectors and other sectors. It will aid the recognition of social tourism if a constructive discourse can be presented and if social tourism partners take parts in events organised by the commercial sectors rather than distancing themselves from them. This does not mean that abuses or mistreatments, or other factors that stand in the way of sustainable and equitable tourism development, should not be challenged and contested.

ISTO today: a powerful network

To carryout its mission, ISTO relies on the strength of its network that comprises more than 160 organisations in almost 40 countries, mainly in Europe and North and South America, but also in Africa.

One of the strengths of ISTO is the diversity of its members, among whom there are not-for-profit associations, cooperatives that manage holiday centres, youth hostel networks and organisations and initiatives for outdoor. Other members are, for example, also travel agencies, unions, cooperation NGOs, educational establishments, local and regional authorities and public tourism organisations that have social tourism activities.

ISTO's activities are mainly focused on providing information, organising events (e.g. the biannual world congress), participating in research and cooperation initiatives and lobbying. These have resulted in a greater recognition of social tourism in international and European organisations.

On the European level, concrete achievements of the last years are as follows.

- The adoption in 2006 of a Opinion on Social Tourism in Europe by the European Economic and Social Committee (EESC) to which ISTO contributed.
- The organisation by the European Commission (Tourism Unit) in partnership with ISTO of a Social Tourism Conference in 2006, 2007 and 2008. This conference focused on highlighting tourism participation figures in Europe and examples of good practice, more specifically in the areas of youth and senior tourism.
- The publication of a study financed by the European Commission about employment in the social tourism sector in Europe [conducted by l'Université Libre de Bruxelles (ULB-IGEAT) for ISTO and the European Federation of Food, Agriculture and Tourism Trade Unions (EFFAT)].
- The adoption by the European parliament of a preparatory action with an allocated budget of €1 million for 2009, with the aim of developing social tourism in Europe.

At the European level, ISTO has also played an innovating role by organising European social tourism forums in Zakopane (2002), Sofia (2003), Riva del Garda (2007) and Malaga (2009). This has allowed social tourism actors in the new Europe to exchange success stories, but also to discuss the challenges in facilitating holiday participation for the greatest number in society.

Even though Europe has been the main focus for ISTO activities, it is important not to forget the other regions in the world.

ISTO have run a division in the Americas since 1994. This division has carried out several research studies and has organised a number of seminars and colloquiums on social tourism and solidarity tourism (Youth tourism in Canada and Mexico, holiday vouchers in Quebec, solidarity tourism and indigenous populations). ISTO Americas has also supported national events dedicated to social tourism (in Mexico, Chile, Canada, Costa Rica etc.).

In 2004, a new division for Africa was created with the aim of developing, where the conditions allow it, social and solidarity tourism on the African continent. A document entitled 'Study on the Concepts and Practices of Social and Solidarity Tourism in Africa' was published in 2007 by ISTO in co-operation with the UNWTO, the French Ministry of Foreign Affairs and the UNAT.

In the future, a division for Asia is being envisioned, as this is an area where ISTO has so far had little presence, despite the growth of the tourism industry there and the potential this offers to enlarge the membership base. The recent collaboration protocol that was signed between the ISTO and the World Leisure Organisation at the latter's 2008 World Congress in Quebec is a first step in this direction.

The growing role of regions and governmental organisations in tourism development has led to the creation in 2006 of a 'Network of Local and Regional Authorities for Social and Solidarity Tourism', which aims to encourage partnership and the exchange of good practices between local and regional actors.

Finally, the ISTO have put in practice a long-standing ambition to promote social tourism accommodation providers via the creation of an online «Tourism for All» portal (www.holidays-for-all.com).

Conclusion

To conclude, this article has confirmed that the social tourism sector is at the core of a humanistic vision for tourism, represents millions of people and is one of the most promising niches of recent years. In Europe, the expansion of the European Union opens up new opportunities. In Latin America, the development potential has become apparent over recent years, and this is an area ISTO wants to actively pursue. As far as Africa and Asia are concerned, it seems that, even if the concept is still largely unknown here, there are several development routes, for example, through cooperative movements and forms of community-based tourism, and the various organisations active in these fields have similar needs as those represented in the social tourism sector. In this context, it can be expected that ISTO will keep profiling itself as an advocate for sustainable, social and solidarity tourism.

Notes

1. This article draws on two articles written by the author in French and published in the journal *Téoros*: Bélanger (1999) and Bélanger (2003). The present article takes into account new developments of recent years and the challenges that present themselves in the decnnium 2010–2020.
2. This topic is discussed in greater depth in a special issue of *Hommes et Migration: Le Temps des Vacances* (N. 1243, May–June 2003).

References

Bélanger, C. (1999). Le tourisme social – Bilan, enjeux et perspectives. *Téoros*, *18*(3), 53–57.
Bélanger, C. (2003). Le Bureau international du tourisme social. *Téoros*, *22*(3), 24–28.
BITS. (1972). *Vienna Charter*. Brussels: Author.
BITS. (1996). *Montreal Declaration, 'Pour une vision humaniste et sociale du tourisme'*. Brussels: Author.
BITS. (2003). *Statutes*. Brussels: Author.

Caire, G., & Rouillet-Caire, M. (2003, September). *Tourisme du Nord et développement durable du Sud: La contribution de l'"alter-tourisme'*. International Forum of Solidarity Tourism (FITS), Marseille, France.

Froidure, J. (1997). *Du tourisme social au tourisme associatif*. Paris: l'Harmattan.

Jolin, L. (2003). Le tourisme social, un concept riche de ses évolutions. *Le tourisme social dans le monde*, Edition spéciale 40ème anniversaire, n. 141

Mignon, J. (2002). *Tendances et défis du tourisme social, BITS International Congress in Mexico City, Conference Proceedings*.

Tonini, N. (2003, September). *L'apport du BITS pour le développement du tourisme solidaire et équitable*. International Forum of Solidarity Tourism (FITS), Marseille, France.

UNAT. (2002). *D'autres voyages du tourisme à l'échange*. Paris: Author.

CASE STUDY

The development of social tourism in Brazil

Marcelo Vilela de Almeida

School of Arts, Sciences and Humanities, University of São Paulo, Rua Arlindo Bettio, 1000, São Paulo/SP 03828-000, Brazil

This article reflects on the origins and development of social tourism in Brazil, with particular reference to the socio-economic conditions in the country. It discusses the theoretical conceptualisation of social tourism and its implementations in the non-European context. The case study presented here is based on a secondary bibliographical research of existing definitions and an in-depth analysis of the political conditions that have framed its development. More particularly, this article will discuss public initiatives since the Labour Party gained power in Brazil in 2003. Apart from public sector involvement in social tourism, this article also examines the role of the third sector in provision. The example of Social Service of Commerce will be presented. This article will conclude by evaluating the phenomenon of social tourism in Brazil, highlighting where progress has been made and which are the key challenges that need to be overcome.

Introduction

One of the most relevant causes for the development of tourism was undoubtedly the introduction of the Holiday with Pay Convention in the twentieth century, which provided workers with a right to time for rest, for family life and for other advantages that can be seen to contribute to the formation of citizenship. Because of this increase in available leisure time, the government, political parties and associations began to focus on how vacation was organised. Once the issue of free time had been solved, there were others such as the lack of money and the dearth of tourism facilities. It was then that social tourism developed as a solution for these problems.

In Brazil, however, social tourism is still a fairly recent phenomenon: the private sector has not shown great interest for this segment, and the public sector has not effectively promoted social tourism in the country – although it is considered a potential solution for the leisure of disadvantaged populations. This can be attributed to the chronic inefficiency of a considerable part of the official Brazilian tourism sector. However, the Brazilian Constitution states in its article 180 that 'the Country, the States, the Federal District and the Cities will promote and will stimulate tourism as a factor for social and economic development' (Brasil, 1988, p. 106). In practice, this consists of a set of actions that are mostly isolated, for instance, the initiatives of entities such as the Social Service of Commerce (SESC)

– this is an organisation run by employees from the commerce and services sector, which is active throughout the country.

This case study article argues that the lack of an adequate understanding of the term 'social tourism' is one of the reasons for its practice being insipient or little known. As a result, the market has taken advantage of a politically desirable, though unclear, goal. Social sustainability and a concern for the community are often seen as a marketing strategy, rather than as an objective *per se*, by companies, unions and other entities. The aim of this article is to describe and analyse the development of social tourism in Brazil, focusing on the initiatives of the public (federal) and the third sector, with particular reference to the example of SESC.

Understanding the meaning of social tourism in the Brazilian context

Although some scholars, such as Haulot (1991), take the several definitions given to the term as a minor matter for discussions, we believe that the simple act of importing definitions that come from foreign literature, without searching for a definition that is more suitable for the Brazilian reality, has contributed to the fact that until recently little progress was made in this area in Brazil. For Boullón (1990, p. 80), 'social tourism and its development in Latin America have been spreading for the last decades, although it had been based on distinct interpretations that do not present any kind of coherence among themselves'. This seems to confirm the fact that the term's lack of clarity on a conceptual level has severely hampered its practical implementation. On the basis of an exhaustive compilation of existing definitions, and accepting the limitations of its current practical applicability in Brazil, this article proposes the following definition:

> Social tourism is socio-politically promoted by the State and organised by civil (commercial and third sector) entities with aims clearly defined for psychophysical recovery and socio-cultural development for individuals, according to the assumptions of sustainability, which must be extended to the places visited. (Almeida, 2001, p. 128)

In the development of a definition for the Brazilian context, it was deemed important to assign the State as a coordinator and a promoting agent of the necessary actions for the development of social tourism. The definition also highlights the involvement of the private sector in the operation of tourism practices at rates that are compatible with their costs, and the role of the third sector. These partners are responsible for the definition of suitable programmes for beneficiaries.

Brazilian governmental action in the social tourism field

In 1966, the first federal governmental institutions were created to coordinate the actions concerning tourism in Brazil. It was through executive order 55, from 18 November that *Empresa Brasileira de Turismo* (EMBRATUR),[1] and also a national policy concerning the sector was established (EMBRATUR, 2006, p. 34). This policy did not mention social tourism, but it focused mainly on attracting foreign tourists to Brazil. It was only in September 1975, with the Tourism National Plan, that the Brazilian government initially showed interest in social tourism, via the establishment of a range of tourism initiatives for social groups living on a minimum wage. This meant that Brazilians in this group of low earners (at that time this corresponded to 80% of the Brazilian population)[2] would be offered programmes and leisure activities in their own neighbourhoods as well as social tourism (campings, leisure camps administered by public bodies, hostels or school facilities that could be used as lodging) (EMBRATUR, 1975, p. 117). Other groups who earned slightly more could make use of campings, leisure camps and/or holiday villas administered by professional associations or semi-governmental bodies.

The above-mentioned plan may have mentioned social tourism initiatives, but it had almost no practical effect. However, some state and municipal governments and some organisations such as unions were providing social tourism, with very limited connections to the federal government. In the 1980s, there were further policy references to social tourism, but, once again, these had very little practical impact:

- In September 1982, EMBRATUR published a document called: *Subsídios para um Programa Nacional de Turismo Social* (subsidies for a National Program of Social Tourism), mentioned by Santos (1993, p. 137).
- Although EMBRATUR's 7th president Joaquim Affonso Mac Dowell Leite de Castro (1985–1986) stated that he would 'invest in so called social tourism, with the creation of packages and programs in order to stimulate the middle class' (EMBRATUR, 2006, p. 64), once more few of these were actually established. The most visible action of social tourism at that time – though the effects were never researched – was the creation of a legal deliberation, number 115 of 5 July 1983.[3] It was the result of a protocol of intentions settled between the Ministry of Labor and EMBRATUR aiming at the introduction of the PNTS (*Política Nacional de Turismo Social do Trabalhador* – in English: a National Policy of Social Tourism for the worker) (Santos, 1993, p. 149).
- In January 1986, during the New Republic era, the proposal for a Tourism National Policy was amended. It included, among its goals between 1986 and 1989, the introduction of social and leisure tourism facilities, in order to serve the 1-day tourism demand generated by the low-income population (EMBRATUR, 1986). This measure was not put into practice, but it is a good indicator of how social tourism was understood at the time.
- Between 1986 and 1988 when João Dória Junior was the president of EMBRATUR, some initiatives were taken place in order to expand domestic tourism.[4] Some of them were: *Passaporte Brasil* (Brazilian Passport: a domestic tourism programme that offered some discounts on trips within the country), *Passaportezinho Brasil* (Brazilian Little Passport: a programme that stimulated domestic tourism for children), tourism programmes aimed at citizens with disabilities, Youth Hostel programmes and the introduction of seniors clubs (EMBRATUR, 2006, p. 68).

The beginning of the 1990s was not a promising time for social tourism. Overall, Brazilian tourism evolved in many aspects. Many of the actions proposed by the *Política Nacional de Turismo* (Tourism National Policy), 1996–1999 were not put into practice – among them there were ones related to the democratisation of domestic tourism, such as: *Calendário de Dias Azuis* (Blue Days Calendar – related to low season days), seniors' clubs, hostels, social tourism for workers, students tourism, etc. (Brasil, 1996, p. 22). This scenario continued until the end of Fernando Henrique Cardoso's second term of office.

The current Brazilian federal government (since 2003) has taken a number of steps in the area of social tourism – even if its actions in this area are modest, they can be seen as potentially more concrete than others in the past. The Ministry of Tourism[5] (MTur) has formed the Thematic Chamber of Segmentation, composed by the Thematic Technical

Groups (GTT in Portuguese), and in 2003, the GTT Social Tourism was created. The activities of the GTT Social Tourism were mostly driven by the discussion of a potential definition for social tourism, which would form the basis for the formulation of policies in this field, as well as by the analysis of social tourism provision in the country. Such discussions led to a set of publications entitled 'Tourism Segmentation – Conceptual Marks', which defined social tourism not as a segment, but as a 'way' of practising tourism, which can be manifested in a variety of the identified segments.

Moreover, the National Plan for Tourism 2003–2007 aimed, in its specific objectives, to democratise tourism participation in a national context – this objective was not explicitly linked to social tourism development, however. Another initiative of MTur is Senior Travel, which aims to facilitate and stimulate travel for Brazilians who are older than 60[6] throughout the Brazilian territory during the low season, via specially developed packages that are exclusively offered to this target group. This initiative was based on *Vacaciones Tercera Edad*, a programme by the Tourism National Service of Chile (Sernatur). The project also offers discounts for those who just look for restaurant offers in the same destinations. Apart from offering tourism products at promotional rates, the project allows retired and public sector workers to build up credit from the Social Security National Institute (INSS), via installments directly withdrawn from their monthly income. These go into their personal bank accounts and are taxed below 1% per month. However, participants in this scheme were not spread equally throughout the country due to the difficulty in transportation and/or to the elevated costs of transportation and/or, at times, to the insufficient demand for it. This has meant that no travel agencies were found to put this offer into practice in some areas.

Nevertheless, the senior travel scheme has proven to be a big success. In 2007, according to MTur and *Panrotas* (tourism media) figures, 9000 packages were sold between August and November, 30% more than the established target. In 2008, the programme projected the sales of 50,000 packages and it was exceeded more than threefold: from March until November, 180,000 trips were sold (Castro, 2009). Besides the packages, the MTur has also launched a programme called *Viaja Mais Melhor Idade Hospedagem* (Seniors Travel More Lodging). It consists of a 50% discount in hotel room rates that are part of the programme for people over 60 years old. This programme was created in order to assist the low occupancy rate of destinations and also to promote leisure and quality of life to elderly citizens. More than 2000 lodgings in 410 destinations were part of the programme in 2009.

Finally, there are two recent initiatives that are worth mentioning with regards to social tourism in Brazil: the financing of tourism packages by *Caixa Econômica Federal* (CEF – a Brazilian state-owned bank) and the launching of *Viaja Mais Jovem* (Travel More – Young People). In April 2009, a protocol of intentions was signed between CEF, MTur and the Brazilian Association of Travel Agencies (ABAV). This protocol offers a financing scheme specifically for tourism: a maximum credit of R$10,000 is available over 24 months. Interest rates are negotiated with each partner, based on regional aspects and on the policies of each participant. A raise of 5% in the tourism business was expected and also in one concerning domestic tourism, specifically 20%. According to the MTur, such credits are aimed at ~20% Brazilians who have been in the consumer's market for the last few years (Albuquerque, 2009). The programme *Viaja Mais Jovem* was launched in May 2008. Its aim was to provide students and teachers with access to tourism experiences during the low season. The pilot focused on 6th grade students (elementary school) of Acre (a state in Brazil). It was a partnership between the Ministry and the State government, with the support of the Education secretary and the Tourism secretary. The MTur and the government of Acre intended to invest R$400,000 on the pilot, which provided free study trips to 600 students and 45 teachers of public schools within the state (Panrotas, 2008). After this experience, the project would be established in Brasilia (Federal District), where it would be extended to 1040 7th grade students of the elementary school and the second year of high school (Souza, 2009).

It is clear from these examples that in the latest period, a series of concrete actions have been put in place to make social tourism a reality in Brazil, as opposed to previous efforts, which yielded very few results. A number of conditions need to be highlighted, however:

- The GTT Social Tourism was planned but never established.
- Much data about the results of the programmes and projects mentioned above are not available yet. It makes the evaluation of the targets difficult, and there is no clear picture yet of their social and economic impacts.
- Part of the tourism trade is still reticent concerning the programmes and projects mentioned: travel agents and users criticised the lack of specific guidelines for the programmes and the facilities that were to be put in place for the senior traveller programme. There was a difficulty in finding specialists for this field who were not involved in commercial provision yet.
- Because there is no specific social tourism policy, the connections between different programmes are often unclear. A more integrated and consistent development of social tourism is needed – at present, social tourism is too often used as a synonym for domestic tourism.

The role of the third sector in the development of social tourism in Brazil: the example of SESC

This section will focus on the role of third sector partners in public social tourism programmes. The impacts of participation in social tourism initiatives will also be explored. The term 'third sector' will be used as discussed by Cardoso (2000):

> The concept of 'Third Sector' itself, its profile and its shapes are not that clear yet, not even for most actors involved in its formation. There are several terms that we have been using to characterize this space, which is nor State nor market and which actions aim at public interest: non-profitable, philanthropic, volunteer interests. [...] I am convinced that the concept of 'Third Sector' describes a space for experiments of new ways of thinking and acting upon the social reality. Its assurance has the great merit of interrupting the dichotomy between public and private, in which public was a synonym for state-owned and private companies. We are witnessing the appearance of a public sphere that is not state-owned and which private initiatives present public sense. This makes social dynamics richer and more complex. (Cardoso, 2000, pp. 7–8)

SESC is a suitable example of this type of organisation. SESC has been active in social tourism in Brazil since 1940, and its services have become reference points for the country. The origin of organisations such as SESC[7] was in 1945, when Brazilian entrepreneurs in the fields of industry, commerce and agriculture gathered in Teresópolis (Rio de Janeiro state). They discussed the future direction of these activities in the country and proposed recommendations in order to improve the conditions and lives of the population. The opening of the holiday centre *Colônia de Férias Rui Fonseca* in 1948, in Bertioga (city by the sea in São Paulo state), represents a milestone at the beginning of SESC's work in the area of leisure and social tourism. It emphasised the importance of free time and wellness, and it served as a model for several camps around the country and as a foundation for the organisation of social tourism programmes not only at SESC São Paulo, but in other states also.

The programme of social tourism of SESC aims at minimising the influence of income on participation in tourism, '[. . .] providing to the commerce worker and his/her dependents an opportunity to travel combined with an offer of meaningful cultural, social and recreational activities' (SESC São Paulo, 1997, p. 185). Thus, through SESC, it is possible to participate in domestic and international tourism and to stay at several camps and lodgings around the country. SESC does not only strive to reduce the price of the holidays and the hotel rates for its members, but above all it aims to transform people by '[. . .] developing their intellectual and physical skills, knowledge and social interaction' (SESC São Paulo, 2006, p. 23). This is achieved through a set of activities planned with this goal in mind. Ethical and sustainable business practices are adhered to.

This example illustrates the way social tourism has been implemented in practice in Brazil over the last 60 years and can be used as a model for further development. Through its organic development, it ensures that the business model followed here is suitable for this particular national context – hence, it could be a basis for the conceptualisation of social tourism in Brazil.

Conclusions

This article has highlighted the conceptual interpretations and policy implementations of social tourism in Brazil. It has shown that the definitions used were often imported from other geographical contexts and need to be adapted to the socio-economic situation in Brazil. It has also shown that in recent decades, social tourism has been mentioned in policy initiatives, but that the political ones will turn these policy mentions into practice has often been lacking. Added to that, there has been some unwillingness in the tourism sector, where the unclear definition of social tourism may have been used as an excuse to not to get involved.

Social tourism could be considered as one of the 'transgressor' leisure activities proposed by Parker (1978, pp. 57–58) – those that can make a big difference by the socially dissatisfied, by those who search for a new identity, for the experiment of new sensations, for more elevated experiences (as the ones proposed by SESC), as opposed to the more conventional leisure activities.

Even if the results of the programmes promoted by the Brazilian government are in need of specific and deepened evaluation, one can ask if it was not reasonable to expect more in terms of inclusion of those who have traditionally been absent from the Brazilian tourism and of a government that has, as its most important representative, a man who prides himself on his knowledge and experience of this group in society. Despite the current economic situation and the measures that have been taken, there is still a big part of the population excluded from the possibilities of tourism. A new social tourism can be a part of a new Brazilian society. With the aid of the third sector, further progress in this field may be realised in the future.

Notes

1. The most important public body of Brazilian tourism up to 2003 when the MTur was established (which this organisation is reporting to). EMBRATUR had its denomination changed into *Instituto Brasileiro de Turismo* (Brazilian Institute of Tourism) in 1991; but the acronym remains.

2. A figure that expresses the inequality of wealth distribution in Brazil.
3. Annulled by Legal Deliberation number 280, from 11 July 1990.
4. Although the source is not clear about social tourism, it is not difficult to notice which kinds of public it meant to reach (children, young people and seniors). And they easily fit into this segment.
5. It was created in 2003, during the first command of President Luiz Inácio Lula da Silva.
6. According to the MTur, this segment represents at least nine million people who can travel. The original name in Portuguese is: *Viaja Mais Melhor Idade*.
7. These organisations are part of what is commonly called the 'S' system, which includes the representative bodies of the industry (SESI and SENAI), commerce and services (SESC and SENAC), agriculture (SENAR), transportation (SEST and SENAT), and from the micro and the small company (SEBRAE).

References

Albuquerque, F. (2009). *Caixa financiará pacotes turísticos nacionais de até R$ 10 mil*. Retrieved from http://www.agenciabrasil.gov.br/noticias/2009/04/27/materia.2009-04-27.6477627855/.

Almeida, M.V. (2001). *Turismo social – por uma compreensão mais adequada deste fenômeno e sua implicação prática na realidade atual brasileira* (Master's Thesis). Brazil: School of Communications and Arts, University of São Paulo.

Boullón, R.C. (1990). *Las actividades turísticas e recreacionales; el hombre como protagonista*. México D.F.: Trillas.

Brasil (1988). *Constituição da República Federativa do Brasil de 1988*. São Paulo: Encyclopaedia Britannica do Brasil.

Brasil (1996). Ministério da Indústria, Comércio e Turismo. *Política nacional de turismo 1996–1999*. Brasília, D.F.

Cardoso, R. (2000). Fortalecimento da sociedade civil. In E.B. Ioschipe (Ed.), *3° setor; desenvolvimento social sustentado* (2nd ed., pp. 7–12). São Paulo: Gife; Paz e Terra (org.).

Castro, R.A. (2009). *Programa Viaja Mais Melhor Idade ganha novo site*. Retrived from http://www.panrotas.com.br/noticia-turismo/mercado/programa-viaja-mais-melhor-idade-ganha-novo-site_50907.html.

EMBRATUR. (1975). *Plano nacional de turismo*. Brasília D.F.

EMBRATUR. (1986). *Política nacional de turismo; proposta*. Brasília D.F.

EMBRATUR. (2006). *EMBRATUR 40 anos*. Brasília D.F.

Haulot, A. (1991). *Turismo social*. México D.F.: Trillas.

Panrotas (2008). *Marta Suplicy lança o Viaja Mais Jovem*. Retrieved from http://www.panrotas.com.br/noticia-turismo/politica/marta-suplicy-lanca-o-viaja-mais-jovem_37607.html.

Parker, S. (1978). Tradução por Heloisa Toller Gomes. *A sociologia do lazer*. Rio de Janeiro: Zahar Editores.

Santos, R.F. (1993). *Turismo social; propostas para seu incremento no Brasil* (Final graduation paper). Department of Public Relations, Publicity and Propaganda, and Tourism. School of Communications and Arts, University of São Paulo.

SESC São Paulo. (1997). *Uma idéia original; SESC São Paulo 50 anos*. São Paulo.

SESC São Paulo. (2006). *Turismo no SESC SP; turismo para todos*. São Paulo: SESC São Paulo.

Souza, A. (2009). *Alunos de Brasília são beneficiados pelo Viaja Mais Jovem*. Retrieved from http://www.panrotas.com.br/noticia-turismo/mercado/alunos-de-brasilia-sao-beneficiados-pelo-viaja-mais-jovem_52870.html.

Index

Page numbers in **bold** represent Figures

Abdullah, J.: and Gilbert, D. 90
accessibility 89–102
Accessible Social Tourism 90–1, 100
Acre 114–15
active ageing 90, 100
adaptation model 5–10, 15
adventure holidays 50, 55
Africa 108–9
Age Concern 55
Albany Lodge 56
All Party Parliamentary Group on Social
  Tourism 2
Almeida, M. 4, 13, 111–17
Anglo-Saxon social model 12
annual holiday access 40
Arthritis Care 55
Asia 109
Association for Equitable and Solidarity
  Tourism (ATES) 107
Aubagne en Provence 105
Australia 81
Austria 25

BAGFE (Bundesarbeitsgemeinschaft
  Familienerholung) 27
Beeton, R.: Hardy, A. and Pearson, L. 16
Bélanger, C.: and Jolin, L. 3–4, 9, 103–10
Belgium 9, 14, 21–2, 25–8, 30, 36, 43, 81
Berkman-Syme Social Network Index 94, 97,
  98, 100
Berlin, I. 12
Bertioga (Brazil) 115
Big Society concept 5
Boullón, R. 112
Brasilia 115
Brazil 2–4, 6, 13, 111–17
Brazilian Association of Travel Agencies
  (ABAV) 114
Brazilian Constitution 111
Brazilian government 112–16
Brazilian social tourism development 111–17;
  governmental action 112–15; third sector
  115–16; understanding context 112

Break (charity UK) 8
Brussels 3, 21
Budapest 69
Bureau International du Tourisme Social
  (BITS) 3–4, 21, 62, 103–4
Butlins 57

Caire, G. 28
Caixa Econômica Federal (CEF) 114
Calendário de Dias Azuis (Blue Days
  Calendar) 113
Calypso programme 13–14, 19, 24, 30, 37,
  90–1
Cameron, Prime Minister David 5
capitalism 22
Cardoso, F. 113
Cardoso, R. 115
Carretero, S.: Garcés, J. and Ferri, M. 3, 89–
  102
Castro, J. 113
Central Eastern Europe 73
Centre for Holiday Participation 8
Charities Digest 52
charity 3, 8, 13, 25–8, 47–60, 69;
  accommodation provision 56, 56;
  fundraising 48–50, 54–5; organisational
  profiles 52, 53; study findings 52–7; study
  methodology 51–2; tourism-charity
  relationship 49–54; understanding charity
  sector 48–9
Charity Commission 59
Charter of Vienna 105
Chauvin, J. 27
Chèques-Vacances (Holiday Vouchers) 8
Children's Adventure Farm Trust (CAFT)
  54–5
Children's Wish Foundation 52
Chile 99
Chunn, D.: and Gavigan, S. 12
citizenship 111
Claire Sadler Trust 54
Clarke, J.: and Critcher, C. 78
Clough, J. 50

commercial tourism 14–15, 19–32
Commission of the European Communities 77
Commissioner for Enterprise and Industry 23
Committee of Regions on Social Tourism 22
community-based tourism 9, 15
cooperative sector 107
Corporate Social Responsibility 3, 8, 48, 56, 58
Cousins, J. 50
Couveia, A. 21
Critcher, C.: and Clarke, J. 78
cultural variation 84, 86
Current Issues in Tourism 1–2, 6

daily routines 77–88
decision-makers 87
Democratic Republic of Germany (GDR) 21–2
deprivation 82; indicators 40; material 77, 87
'desert' concept 12
developing countries 50, 104
Diekmann, A.: and McCabe, S. 2, 12
Disability Discrimination Act (DDA 1995) 56
Disability Foundation 54–5
disabled people 21–23
disadvantaged groups 1–11, 15, 21–7, 34–5, 41, 47–73, 78, 106, 111; older adults 89–102, *see also* low-income groups
Dória Junior, J. 113

East-Central Europe 63
Eastern Europe 21
economic benefits 3, 7–10, 13–15, 23–4, 35, 39–40, 44, 73–4
Economic and Social Research Council 2
economy 29–30
educational movements 105
employment 2, 9–11, 20–4, 26, 31, 37, 78–9, 84; non-paid work 78–9
Empresa Brasileira de Turismo (EMBRATUR) 112–13
environmental issues 33
Erikson, R. 44
ethics 10–13, 21, 58, 78
EU Survey on Income and Living Conditions (SILC) 34, 38–40
EU Sustainable Development Strategy 37
Europe 2–3, 5–17, 19–32, 36–7, 43, 63, 73, 78, 90–1, 103, 108–9; GDP 89–90; governments 89; social model 11–12
European Commission (EC) 19–39, 44, 90, 108; social tourism understanding 23–4
European Commission for Enterprise and Industry 13
European Economic and Social Committee (EESC) 10, 12–13, 23, 33–6, 108

European Federation for Food Agriculture and Tourism (EFFAT) 20, 108
European Ministerial Conference 36
European Parliament 108
European Strategy (2020) 90
European Union 1, 6, 19–46, 69, 77–8, 87, 89, 109; Belgian Presidency (2001) 36; Member States 90; social tourism systems 19–32
European Union systems 19–32; accessibility 28–9, **29**; European Commission's understanding 23–4; funding 25–6; social tourism definition 21–3; supply and facilities 27; target groups 26–7
European Year of Equal Opportunities for All (2007) 24
Evans, M.: and Kelley, J. 80

Fáilte Ireland (National Tourism Development Authority) 38
family centres 27
Family Fund (FF) 51
Family Holiday Association (FHA) 25, 27, 47, 50–1, 54–6
family market 106
Federation of International Youth Travel Organisations (FIYTO) 21
Federation of Popular Travel Organisations (IFPTO) 21
Ferri, M.: Carretero, S. and Garcés, J. 3, 89–102
Flanders (Belgium) 8, 10, 43
France 8, 10, 14–15, 20, 22, 25–8, 30, 36, 43, 66, 73, 78, 90, 106–7
free competition 105
functional health 89–102
funding 21–2, 25–6; public 1, 22, 25–6, 30; state 64–5, **65**

Garcés, J.: Carretero, S. and Ferri, M. 3, 89–102
Gavigan, S.: and Chunn, D. 12
General Assembly in Vienna (1972) 105
George, R. 11
Germany 21–2, 25, 27–8, 62
Gilbert, D.: and Abdullah, J. 90; Miller, G. and Turner, R. 47–51, 55, 57–8
global economic crisis 73
Global Tourism Code of Ethics 104
good cause giving 49
Graburn, N. 54
Griffin, K.: and Stacey, J. 3, 13, 33–46

Hall, C. 34
Hardy, A.: Beeton, R. and Pearson, L. 16
Haukeland, J. 78
Haulot, A. 10, 21, 35, 112

health 77–87; benefits 3, 89–109; cognitive status 94, 96–100, *97*; functional capacity 94–6, 99–100; home help service *99*, 100; older adults 89–102, *96*, *97*; services 95–100, *98*, *99*; systems 90

healthy ageing 89–102; study methodology 91–5, *92*; study results 95–9

Higgins, M.: and Smith, W. 49

Holiday Care Service 57

holiday centres 14, 28, 63, 115

Holiday Cheque Plus Sale 72

holiday cheque system (HCS) 66–74, **68**, *70*, **70**, **71**, **72**

Holiday with Pay Convention 104, 111

holiday vouchers 8, 25, 26, 63

holidaying 34–43, 52–5, 61, 90–1, 106; acknowledging value 40; constraints 57; non-participation 35; societal norm 77–88

Hoseasons 57

host community 13–15, 24, 105–6

Hotel Association of Hungary 73

Hughes, H. 35; and Smith, V. 47, 51, 58, 87

human rights 36, 48, 61, 74, 103–10

Hungarian Central Statistical Office 62

Hungarian government 66, 69, 73–4

Hungarian National Foundation of Recreation (HNFR) 66–74

Hungarian Parliament 73

Hungarian social tourism 61–75; after (1989) 66–7; current HCS 67–9; development 63–6, **64**, **65**; holiday cheque use 69–73, **71**; present and future 73–4; state funding **65**; tourism industry 62–3

Hungary 3, 8, 61–75

Hunguest Corporation 66–9

Hunguest Hotels 65–9

Hunter-Jones, P. 3, 13, 47–60

Hunzicker, W. 6, 9, 21

hypercompetitiveness 105

ideology 62–3, 105

illness stress 99

immigrant groups 106

IMSERSO (Institute of Elderly and Social Services) programme 9, 26–8, 90, 99

inclusion model 5–10, 15

income equality 84

independent activities of daily life (IADL) 94–100

inequality 11–13, 20, 77–88, 105

infrastructure 14, 22, 73, 104

Institute of Geography (Pécs University) 72

integrated supply approach 42–3

intellectual capacity 100

international community 104

International Covenant on Economic Social and Cultural Rights 104

International Forum of Solidarity Tourism (FITS) 107

international network 107

International Social Survey Programme (ISSP) 3, 80–2; Leisure and Sports module (2007) 81

International Social Tourism Organisation (ISTO) 3–4, 9, 14, 20, 22, 103–10; current objectives 106–8; resources 107–8; social tourism actor 103–4; social tourism development 104–5; today's network 108–9

Ireland 1, 3, 13, 21; 'tourism for all' policy 33–46

Irish government 3, 39

Irish tourism sustainability 33–46; conceptualising 'tourism for all' 34–5; European level 36–7; policy 35–9; social exclusion 35; sustainability 37–8

ISTO Americas 106–9

Italian Association for Responsible Tourism (AITR) 107

Italy 36, 107

Jafari, J. 16

Japan 83–4, 86

Jolin, L.: and Bélanger, C. 3–4, 9, 103–10

Joseph Rowntree Charitable Trust 51

K&H Bank 73

Kelley, J.: and Evans, M. 80

Labour Party (Brazil) 111

Labour and social Affairs Ministry (Spain) 26

Lake Balaton 69

Länder social ministry 25

Latin America 109, 112

Lawton & Brody Index 94, 96, *97*

Lisbon strategy 24, 37

Livability 55–6

long-term care (LTC) 89–90, 98

low-income groups 9, 41, 51, 62, 77–80, 87, 90, 104, 112–13

McCabe, S. 1, 13, 90; and Diekmann, A. 2, 12; *et al* 90

Macmillan Cancer Trust 54, 56

Maitland, R.: Minnaert, L. and Miller, G. 1–17, 21, 28, 51

Malcolm Sargent fund 51

Manila Declaration (1980) 61, 104

Margate (UK) 50–1

Maurin, E. 28

Maynard, P. 2

memory 100

mental health 99

Mexico 106

Mexico City 106

Miller, G.: Gilbert, D. and Turner, R. 47–51, 55, 57–8; Maitland, R. and Minnaert, L. 1–17, 21, 28, 51
Ministry of Tourism (MTur Brazil) 113–14
Ministry of Labor (Brazil) 113
Ministry of Public Welfare (Hungary) 66
Minnaert, L. 13; Maitland, R. and Miller, G. 1–17, 21, 28, 51; and Schapmans, M. 87
Montreal Declaration on Social Tourism (1996) 22, 103, 105–7; Addendum of Aubagne (2006) 103, 105
Multiple Sclerosis Society 55
Mundt, J. 21

National Action Plan for Social Inclusion (Ireland 2007–2016) 34
National Council of Trade Unions (NCTU) 64
National Development Plan (Ireland 2007–2013) 34
National Holiday and Property Handling Limited Co. 66
National House of Pensions and Health Insurances (CNPAS) 25–6
National Lottery 49
National Plan for Tourism (Brazil 2003–2007) 114
National Play Policy (2004–2008) 41
National Sustainable Development Strategy (Ireland) 38
Nawijn, J. 79; *et al* 79
negative liberty 12
neo-liberalism 24, 29
NET-STaR (Network for Social Tourism and Regeneration) 2
New Horizons Strategy for Irish Tourism (2003–2012) 38
non-disadvantaged groups 7
non-governmental organisations (NGOs) 39–43, 107
Norway 83–4, 86

Opinion on Social Tourism in Europe 108
Organisation for Economic Cooperation and Development (OECD) 38
Over the Wall 52

paid annual holidays 78
Palma conference 22
Panrotas (tourism media) 114
Parker, S. 116
participation model 5–10, 15
Pearson, L.: Beeton, R. and Pearson, L. 16
personal liberty 12
Pfeiffer, E. 97, *97*
philanthropic principles 48

PNTS (*Politica Nacional de Turismo Social do Trabalhador*) 113
Poland 26–7
Polibienestar Research Institute (Valencia University) 93
policy 1, 19–32, 103–16; development 39–42; partnership approach 41–2; social strategy 89–102; 'tourism for all' 33–46
policy-makers 39–40, 44
positive liberty 12
poverty 9, 28, 33–5, 38, 40, 43, 51
private sector 8, 30, 47–9, 106, 112
pro-poor tourism initiatives 9, 15
product development 106
public sector 1, 4, 13, 21, 48, 106, 111; intervention 42
public welfare 5–6
Puzcó, L.: and Rátz, T. 3, 8, 61–75

Quinn, B.: *et al* 90

Rátz, T.: and Puzcó, L. 3, 8, 61–75
reference group 80, 84
regeneration strategy 2
relationships 100
Renewed Tourism Policy 23
research facilitator 51
respite breaks 25, 54, 57
Richards, G. 38
Romania 25–7
Romanian government 73
Royal National Institute for the Blind (RNIB) 56

São Paulo 116
Schapmans, M.: and Minnaert, L. 87
seasonality 24, 31, 36–7
self-perceived health 99
Sen, G. 80
senior citizens 7–10, 14, 24–7, 89–102, 114; autonomy 100
Senior Travel 114
Short Portable Mental Status Questionnaire (SPMSQ) 94, 97, *97*
signposting 51, 57–8
Sin, H. 50
Smith, V. 35, 40; and Hughes, H. 47, 51, 58, 87
Smith, W.: and Higgins, M. 49
social: benefits 5–17, 35, 39–40, 44; equity 19–32; exclusion 35, 77–82, 86–7, 99; inclusion 10–11, 33–46, 61, 78, 82, 94–100; justice 42; liberalism 29; strata 83–7; systems 21, 107; welfare 36, 63
social care services 91, 95, 98–100
social policy strategy 89–102
Social Security National Institute (INSS) 114

Social Service of Commerce (SESC) 111–12, 115–16
social status 3, 71–2, 78, 86; subjective 79–87, *83, 85*
Social Tourism Conference 108
Social Tourism Declaration 25
social tourism definition 5–17, **7**; ethical justifications 10–13; European perspectives 21–3; interpretations 6–15; socio-economic justifications 13–15
social welfare 12, 30
socialism 61–75, 105
societal norm 77–88; holidaying perception 78–9; social exclusion 79–80; study methodology 80–2; study results 82–6
societal phenomenon 26
society 6–13, 35–7, 50, 61–2, 74, 86–7, 90, 100, 106, 108, 116; affluent 80–1; individualised 11–13; inequality 77–88; Ireland 38; socialised 11–12
solidarity tourism 9, 14–15, 106–9
Spain 9, 26, 28, 43, 89–102, 106
Spanish government 9
sponsored activities 54–5
Stacey, J.: and Griffen, K. 3, 13, 33–46
status symbol 11
stimulation model 5–10, 13, 15
Subsídios para um Programa Nacional de Turismo Social 113
supply and demand 20
supported holiday system 61
sustainability 16, 19–32, 105, 107, 112; challenges 38; Irish tourism 33–46

target groups 26–30, 37, 114
tax 9
Taxation Law (Hungary) 67
technology 49
Teenage Cancer Trust 55
Teresópolis 115
Thematic Chamber of Segmentation 113
Thematic Technical Groups (GTT) 114; GTT Social Tourism 114, 115
third sector 111–12, 115–16
tourism: facilitator 50–1; initiatives 9; participation 48, 78, 99, 104–6
'Tourism for All' (TFA) 9, 22–4, 28, 58, 103–10; agenda 21; conceptualising 34–5; European level 36–7; generating awareness 41; Ireland 33–46; policy perspectives 35–6; sustainability 37–8

tourism industry 8–10, 19, 79, 108; charity involvement framework 50; Hungary 62–3, *63*, 69–73
Tourism National Plan (Brazil 1975) 112–13
Tourism National Service of Chile (Sernatur) 114
Tourism Research Centre (Budapest University) 66
Tourism Sustainability Group (TSG) 22–3, 30
Tourism Unit 24
'Tourismus fü'r alle' 21
trade unions 61–75, **65**
Turner, R.: Gilbert, D. and Miller, G. 47–51, 55, 57–8

UNAT 22
unemployment 26, 28
United Kingdom (UK) 1–3, 5, 8, 13, 20–8, 36, 49–59; charities 47–60; government 5, 26, 40
United Nation's World Tourism Organisation 36–7
United States of America (USA) 12
Universal Declaration of Human Rights 36, 61, 104
Urry, J. 79

Vacaciones Tercera Edad 114
Valencia 89–102
Viaja Mais Jovem (Travel More - Young People) 114
Viaja Mais Melhor Idade Hospedagem 114
volunteerism 50

Web 2.0 technologies 49
welfare tourism 14, 64, 73
Western European model 62
Will, J. 12
Winged Fellowship Trust 52–4
worker movements 27, 104
World Health Organisation (WHO) 90
World Leisure Organisation 109
World Tourism Organisation (UNWTO) 104
World War II 103–4

Ylikännö, M. 3, 77–88
Youth Hostel Association (YHA) 26, 28
youth tourism 8, 24, 27, 106